THE ABSOLUTE BASICS OF THE Wesleyan Way

THE ABSOLUTE + BASICS OF THE Wesleyan WAY

PHIL TALLON
AND
JUSTUS HUNTER

Seedbed

Printed in the United States of America

Illustrations by Andrew Chandler
Cover design and page layout by Nick Perreault at Strange Last Name

Tallon, Philip Christian.
   The absolute basics of the Wesleyan way / Phil Tallon and Justus Hunter. –
Franklin, Tennessee : Seedbed Publishing, ©2020.

      pages : illustrations ; cm.

      Includes bibliographical references.
      ISBN 9781628247725 (paperback)
      ISBN 9781628247763 (DVD)
      ISBN 9781628247756 (updf ebk.)

      1. Methodist Church--Doctrines. 2. Christian life--Methodist authors.
      3. Methodism.   I. Title. II. Hunter, Justus Hamilton, 1982-

BX8331.3.T34 2020   230/.76   2020942639

SEEDBED PUBLISHING
Franklin, Tennessee
seedbed.com

In honor of the student ministry staff at St. Luke's.
Thanks for all you do.

*

In memory of my father,
Rev. H. Wayne Hunter

CONTENTS

ACKNOWLEDGMENTS

As with most things in the Christian life, a supportive community is necessary to do anything worthwhile. This project is no exception. We would like to thank our loving families, who gave us time, space, and encouragement to write. We would also like to thank our church families for the care of our souls and interest in the project.

Kevin Watson at Candler School of Theology, a fine scholar and friend, devoted many hours to reading this manuscript and making suggestions. We owe him many thanks.

Thanks to Seedbed for their vision, guidance, and support of this project. Special thanks are due to Andy Miller, Andrew Dragos, Holly Jones, Nick Perreault, and J. D. Walt. Also, Ryan Staples (kokomofilm.com) is an excellent video editor.

We would especially like to recognize Andrew Chandler, the artist who has graced these pages and the videos with his skill and thoughtfulness. You can find more of his work at andrewchandler.net.

HOW TO USE THIS BOOK

This book has three main elements:

1. There are twelve **lessons** focused on three main aspects of the Wesleyan movement: John Wesley's life, his core theological message, and the legacy of Wesley's leadership on the people called Methodist. These lessons are intended to be short, clear, and to the point. They use big analogies to communicate the big ideas, but not the finer points of Wesley's life and thought. The endnotes point to deeper resources for further study.

2. **Discussion questions** conclude each lesson. They are intended to help readers clarify their understanding of the big ideas, but also to discuss where they are along the way of salvation.

3. There are **endnotes** for those who want to dive deeper into the key ideas. On average, there are about three big notes per lesson.

Anyone can pick up this book and read it on their own, but it is designed for groups to use in discussion of the core elements of the Wesleyan way. If you are using this in a class setting, such as a new member or confirmation class in church, or in a small-group study, here are some suggestions:

The **lessons** are short so that anyone can read through them quickly. Teachers leading students through the material should have everyone read the chapters ahead of time and begin to work on some of the questions so they will be ready for discussion. There are also fun, illustrated videos of the text of the chapters, which are available in Seedbed's online store at store.seedbed.com. When the class gathers together, we suggest showing the videos, then breaking into groups to grapple with

the discussion questions, and then gathering together again to talk about the key points to make sure everyone understands them. If you like this study, you will probably like our prior study as well: *The Absolute Basics of the Christian Faith.* You can also pick it up at Seedbed's online store.

The endnotes provide a more in-depth discussion of the big points. Teachers who are leading students or adults through the material should read these sections so they have a better sense of what's going on behind the scenes; specifically, where to go to read more deeply on the bits of historical or theological complexity. If teachers only want to pick up an additional book or two for background reading, we recommend Henry H. Knight III's *John Wesley: Optimist of Grace* (Cascade, 2018) and Kenneth J. Collins's *The Theology of John Wesley: Holy Love and the Shape of Grace* (Abingdon, 2007). We have also included, as an appendix, John Wesley's classic sermon "The Scripture Way of Salvation" for further study.

THE ABSOLUTE BASICS OF THE Wesleyan WAY

UNIT 1:

WHO WAS JOHN WESLEY?

LESSON 1:

What Was the Young Wesley Like?

"Long my imprisoned spirit lay,
Fast bound in sin and nature's night."

—Charles Wesley, "And Can It Be, That I Should Gain"

John Wesley knew his life had a purpose. He just didn't always know what it was.

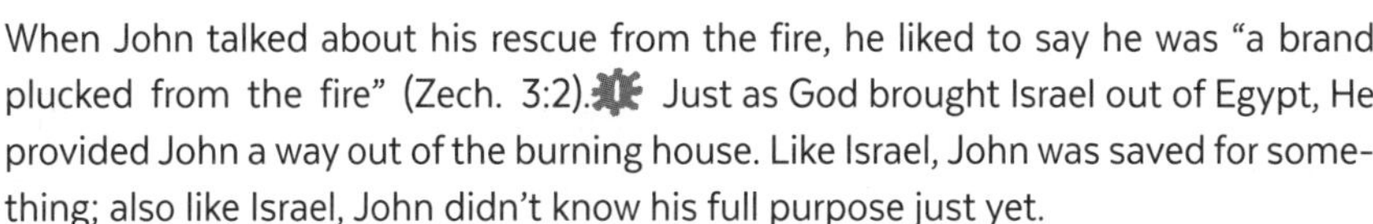

In 1709, when John was five years old, the Wesley family's home caught fire while they slept. His parents, Samuel and Susanna, managed to get John's siblings out of the house, but John was trapped on the second floor. As the house weakened, a neighbor, standing on the shoulders of other men, pulled John from the window before the roof collapsed.

When John talked about his rescue from the fire, he liked to say he was "a brand plucked from the fire" (Zech. 3:2). Just as God brought Israel out of Egypt, He provided John a way out of the burning house. Like Israel, John was saved for something; also like Israel, John didn't know his full purpose just yet.

John grew up well. He was a good son, a good brother, and a good student. In 1720, John went to college at one of the best universities in the world: Oxford. At Oxford, he approached both his studies and his religion very methodically.

John's mother, Susanna, taught him the importance of method. Any time you learn something new, you use a method. A method is an orderly series of steps you take to gain something. The scientific method is an orderly series of steps you take to gain scientific knowledge.

Let's say you want to learn to speak French. You could go to the library and pick a random French book off the shelf, watch a few French films, read a few pages here and there in a French dictionary, and so on. Maybe, if you continued doing random French-ish things for long enough, you would gain some knowledge of the French language. But you wouldn't have your method to thank for it. You would learn *in spite of* your method.

Now imagine you began by enrolling in an introductory French course and you kept records to ensure you spent at least an hour every day working through your introductory French book, never moving ahead unless you had mastered the prior content. And then, after a couple of years of study, you moved to Paris for six months. In this case, chances are good that you would learn to speak French. Why? Because you had a good method.

John was obsessed with having a good method. He believed in the power of method. As a student, this meant the careful study of math, history, languages, and so on. As a Christian, this meant the careful study of his soul.

At Oxford, John and his brother Charles gathered a group of Christians interested in the methodical care of their souls. But this seemed strange to others at the university:

Many began noticing with some alarm what seemed to them to be fanatical practices of fasting on Wednesdays and Fridays, annoying habits such as getting up at four and five o'clock in the morning, and the seemingly radical extent to which Wesley and his friends carried their frugality and their various methods of self-denial.

While classmates were enjoying themselves, John and his friends were reading their Bibles and denying themselves. They were seeking to become holy. John, Charles, and their friends were so committed to the methodical approach to faith that they earned several nicknames at Oxford. Some called them "Bible Moths," while others called them "the Holy Club." There was another name that people called John's group. They meant it as an insult, but John adopted it as a badge of honor: the "Methodists."

The Wesley brothers' methodical faith led them to travel to Georgia as missionaries. As their voyage began in October 1735, John kept up his methodical pursuit of the faith. At sea, he settled for a simple diet of rice and bread. Each day he spent an hour in private prayer, an hour in public prayer, and two hours in the study of Scripture—all before 9:00 a.m.!

In all likelihood, Wesley took his faith more seriously than you or I. Despite all this, there was still something missing. His methods weren't enough.

In the 1700s, it took several months to sail across the Atlantic Ocean from England to America. In late January 1736, while still at sea, the weather turned bad. Several storms threatened the Wesleys' ship, the *Simmonds*. Each time, John was terrified. Instead of trusting in God, he was terrified at the possibility of his own death.

Jesus Christ slept while the storm raged (Mark 4:37–40), but John Wesley trembled in fear.

The worst storm kicked up on January 25, during a worship service on board the *Simmonds.* While Wesley and the English passengers trembled, the Germans on board the ship sang hymns. Wesley wrote:

> The sea broke over, split the mainsail in pieces, covered the ship, and poured in between the decks, as if the great deep had already swallowed us up. A terrible screaming began among the English. The Germans calmly sang on. I asked one of them afterward, "Were you not afraid?" He answered, "I thank God, no." I asked, "But were your women and children not afraid?" He replied mildly, "No; our women and children are not afraid to die." ✷

John was so moved by the example of the German Christians that he questioned how real his own faith was. If his faith could not stand in the face of the ultimate test—death—what sort of faith was it?

In early February, the Wesleys arrived in Georgia. John became an Anglican priest in Savannah.

However, John's ministry in Georgia did not meet his expectations. He had hoped to bring the gospel to Indigenous Peoples. But when the task became difficult, he gave up.

Worst of all was the ordeal with Sophia Hopkey. One of John Wesley's responsibilities, as an Anglican priest, was to oversee Communion in his church. Not only did he lead the Communion service, he also ensured that only people who were properly prepared received the bread and wine.

Unsurprisingly, John developed a method for this responsibility. Those who prepared themselves by prayer, fasting, and confession of sin were allowed to receive Communion.

He even scheduled time every Saturday for people to come for prayer and confession, to make sure they were prepared. These rules were not entirely unusual for Wesley's day. What really got him in trouble was how strict he could be in deciding who had properly confessed their sins.

John developed a close friendship with a young woman in Savannah named Sophia Hopkey. He served as her tutor in the faith and in French. Over time, they fell in love. But John was troubled and indecisive. At moments he was warm with Sophia, and at other moments very cold. Over time, likely from frustration, Sophia decided to marry another man. Wesley was heartbroken.

As a result of the marriage, Sophia stopped attending Communion as regularly. She ceased going to the Saturday night meetings for confession of sin. John became concerned Sophia was not properly prepared to receive Communion.

One Sunday in August 1737, Wesley refused to give Sophia the bread and wine. Sophia was humiliated. In eighteenth-century Georgia, priests who performed their job improperly could be taken to court. Sophia's guardian, a powerful leader in Savannah, charged John with several crimes. Feeling weak and defeated, John abandoned Savannah and set sail back to England.

On his way home, John catalogued his weaknesses in his journal. He lacked faith. He was filled with pride. He still feared death. He was lazy. He often spoke harshly.

Despite the carefulness of his methods, Wesley thought himself a failure.

John Wesley knew his life had a purpose, he just didn't always know what it was. Whatever that purpose was, he didn't find it in Georgia.

In the next lesson, we'll talk about the moment that warmed Wesley's heart and changed the direction of his life.

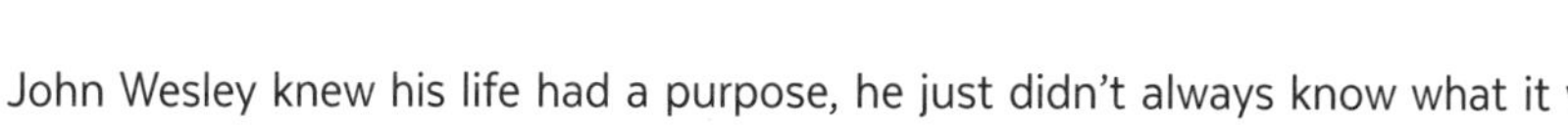

QUESTIONS FOR DISCUSSION

1. Do you know what God's purpose is for you? What have you done to try and fulfill that purpose?

2. What methods have you used to try and become more like Jesus? What was the result? What methods do you think you need to focus on right now?

3. Have you ever felt like John Wesley did in Georgia? Have you ever felt like all your hard work just isn't working?

What Happened at Aldersgate?

"Thine eye diffused a quick'ning ray,
I woke, the dungeon flamed with light;"
—Charles Wesley, "And Can It Be, That I Should Gain"

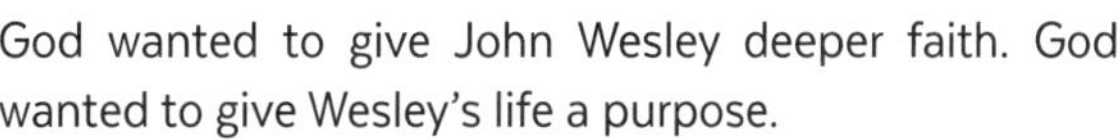

God wanted to give John Wesley deeper faith. God wanted to give Wesley's life a purpose.

When John returned from Georgia, he was confused and uncertain. To his mind, the voyage was a failure. He did not reach the Indigenous Peoples with the gospel. He left the church in Savannah in disgrace.

But the most troubling thing wasn't his outward actions—it was what his failed actions revealed about his inner life. John's mission to Georgia showed him that he still struggled with sin. He was terrified of death, when he should have been trusting in God. He was harsh with others, when he should have been compassionate. He was weak in the face of difficulty, when he should have been strong.

In the book of Romans, Paul says to the Christians at Rome, "You did not receive a spirit of slavery to fall back into fear, but you have received a spirit of adoption" (8:15). Wesley kept falling back in fear. So was he adopted? Was he a child of God? Did he really have faith?

Wesley remained committed to his method of fasting, prayer, and meeting with other Christians, but he knew he needed something more. He knew God was calling him deeper into the faith.

John arrived in England in February 1738. Less than a week after his arrival, he met a man named Peter Böhler. Böhler was a Moravian, just like the group of German Christians who amazed Wesley at sea when they remained calm in the face of violent storms.

The Moravians were very serious about their piety, or holiness. They practiced a simple lifestyle. They gathered together regularly to discuss their faith and pray together in what they called "society meetings." They were leaders in missions. Above all, they lived with deep happiness; they carried peace and joy with them even when their lives were threatened. And their lives were often threatened.

In short, the German Moravians were what the English Methodists wanted to be. They had a method, like John did, but their method was *working*. John Wesley's group was called the Holy Club, but these Moravians were really holy. They were truly happy. They combined their outward actions with inward change.

Wesley learned three key ideas from Böhler. First, Wesley needed *deeper faith*. His terror at sea and harsh judgment of others confirmed his faith was lacking. He needed the perfect love that drives out all fear (1 John 4:18).

Second, Wesley learned that only *God* could give that deeper faith. God wanted to give John a faith that gave him a deep and lasting peace, the kind of faith the German Christians had. But only God could give it; Wesley couldn't create it himself.

Third, Wesley learned the way to deeper faith was *repentance*. Though it was painful, in recognizing his own sinfulness, John was preparing himself for God's gift of deeper faith. The only thing to do was to wait in repentance for God to give him that gift.

John continued his methodical approach to the faith. Böhler and the German Christians confirmed his methodical practices were on track. It was at this time that he also began preaching the Moravian message of deeper faith as the gift of God.

While John was preaching, his brother Charles became quite ill. On May 21, 1738, while Charles was resting, he heard a voice say, "In the name of Jesus of Nazareth, arise, and believe, and you will be healed of all your infirmities." It was the voice of a friend, Mrs. Turner, sitting by his sickbed in prayer. Shortly after her command, Charles felt "a strange palpitation of heart," and received a deep happiness accompanied by a deeper faith. God impressed His love on Charles's heart, and he felt a peace with God and love for others from that day on.

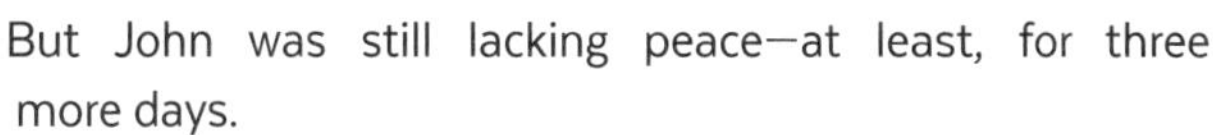

(CHARLES WESLEY)

But John was still lacking peace—at least, for three more days.

On the evening of May 24, John went to Aldersgate Street for a Moravian-style society meeting with his fellow Methodists—a meeting for prayer, spiritual reading, conversation, and confession. He described his experience there as follows:

I went very unwillingly to a society in Aldersgate Street, where one was reading [Martin] Luther's Preface to the Epistle to the Romans. About a quarter before nine, while he was describing the change which God works in the heart through faith in Christ, *I felt my heart strangely warmed.* I felt I did trust in Christ, Christ alone for salvation, and an assurance was given me that he had taken away my sins, even mine, and saved me from the law of sin and death.

Something big happened at Aldersgate. But what happened?

After all, John Wesley was a good Christian boy before Aldersgate. His parents had him baptized in the Church of England. He prayed, fasted, and led others to Christ. He was a priest in the Church of England. He crossed the Atlantic to share the gospel. So what happened at Aldersgate? What was the deeper thing God called John into there?

Wesley talked about his Aldersgate experience in several different ways. One important way John talked about his experience was that, before Aldersgate, he had the *form of godliness.* But at Aldersgate, he gained the *power of God.* What did he mean?

Imagine you like to build remote-controlled cars. You order a new Jeep, and the package comes with all the parts. Included in the package is a set of instructions. They show you the form of the car. You follow those instructions methodically. And the next thing you know, you have arranged all these bars and rods and panels and wheels into the shape, the form, of a car. But the car won't do what it is supposed to do just yet. You need to give it some power. It needs batteries! Only once it has that power can it make use of its form. Only with form and power can the car fulfill its purpose.

The same is true for the Christian life: we need the *form of godliness*—the methods of holy living—and we need the *power of God* to be really holy and truly happy.

Another way of thinking about it is like this: at Aldersgate, John finally discovered his true purpose. He discovered the fullness of life that he was meant for.

Imagine you are a newly hatched baby goose. You think to yourself, *Why do I have these wings? Why do I have this flat bottom, short legs, and webbed feet? Waddling is slow and awkward. Why can't I be sleek and have four legs like the horse?* Then one day you step out on the lake and realize you

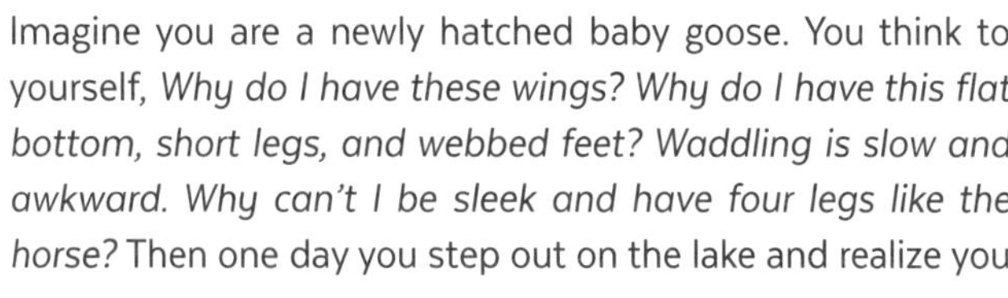

have a flat bottom and two short legs with webbed feet so that you float and paddle smoothly across the water. Your wings lay nice and flat against your body, helping you float and keeping you warm when wet. *That must be what these wings are for,* you think. And now you don't care so much about those two little legs, webbed feet, and flat bottom. You can glide across the water! But little do you realize, there is so much more that you can do with that body. You have the form to fly, but you don't realize it.

Then, you see the older geese start flapping their wings to scoot around the lake and gather more food. And so you start flapping yours. At first, you are just "beating the air," because you don't have the power of flight. But at some point, once your feathers develop and your muscles strengthen, you cross over. You have the form of flight and the power of flight. And now you can glide, not only on water, but on the air! Form and power come together, and you realize what that strange body was for all along. And when you realize what it was for, you realize it isn't strange at all. It's just right. This is why you were created the way you are. This is your purpose.

Salvation is like that. It's when we finally become who we were meant to be.

But there's another piece. Geese find their purpose when they learn to fly. And when they learn to fly they discover they can go further than a baby goose could ever imagine. They can fly for thousands of miles. They can cross whole countries in a few days.

In a similar way, God doesn't only want us to be good. He doesn't only want us to do great things. He wants to give us deep faith so we can go far. He gives us the form of godliness and the power of God so we can become more and more like Jesus than we would ever expect.

God gave John and Charles Wesley deeper faith than they ever expected. And through the power of their faith, God changed the world.

QUESTIONS FOR DISCUSSION

1. Most of the time, do you feel like a slave to sin or like a child of God?

2. Where in your life do you need the power of God to move deeper in your faith?

3. Have you ever felt God moving in you the way that God moved in John and Charles? If so, when was it? If not, what should you do about this?

What Was Wesley Like after Aldersgate?

> "King of glory, soul of bliss, Alleluia!
> Everlasting life is this, Alleluia!
> Thee to know, thy power to prove, Alleluia!
> Thus to sing, and thus to love, Alleluia!"
>
> —Charles Wesley, "Christ the Lord Is Risen Today"

Before Aldersgate, Wesley had the *form* of godliness: he prayed, fasted, baptized, served Communion, and generally did what godly priests do. After Aldersgate, he had the *power* of God. But power doesn't replace form—it *fills* it.

Wesley often described Methodists as those who have, not only the form of godliness, but the power of God. Note the "not only." Lots of things in life need *not only* the form, but also need power.

To be fun, a remote-controlled car needs *not only* the form of a tiny car, it needs batteries as well.

To fly in the sky, a kite needs *not only* the form of a kite, it needs the power of the wind as well.

Or think about it like this: if you buy a house, you buy the *form* of a house. You get the structure. The walls and the roof and the plumbing. But the house is not a home yet. A house doesn't become a home until it's filled up with life.

After you buy the house, you move in your books and towels and refrigerator and beds. You move in all the things you need to live well, and then you call the electric company and have them turn the power on.

Now, it's possible to live without the form of a house. You can even have a lot of the benefits of a home without a house. But it's better to have both. The power of home without a house gets your stuff wet; you need a roof over your head. The form of the house without the power of home gives you a backache; the bare floor is hard. But with both, you can settle in and build a life.

Sometimes people think that the power of God replaces the forms of godliness. They think that as long as you have *power*, the *form* doesn't matter that much. But Wesley shows us that power doesn't replace form. In fact, the power of God made Wesley more passionate about the forms of godliness. More important, it allowed him to understand the forms of godliness better than before. He now understood what they were really for.

This explains why, after Aldersgate, John Wesley still did "form of godliness" stuff. He remained methodical about prayer, Bible study, and gathering with other Christians. He remained committed to the teachings of his church, the Church of England. He was still a priest, so he still preached sermons and led Communion.

John kept detailed diaries of his daily practice. Here's a diary entry for a normal weekday, roughly a year after Aldersgate:

Tuesday, March 20.

[Wesley let himself sleep in this morning after praying past midnight the day before.]

6:45–8:00	Prayed, had tea and religious talk.
8:00–9:00	At home with my brother Charles and others for religious talk.
9:00–11:00	Went to Agutter's for necessary business.
11:00–2:00	Wrote to colleagues James Hervey, to George Whitefield, Seward, Ingham.
2:00–3:00	Went home to take care of necessary business. Mr. Hone came by for religious talk.
3:00–4:15	Went to James Hutton's for religious talk and tea.
4:15–5:00	Went to Mr. Hastings'.
5:00–6:00	Sang, etc. at Mr. Hastings'.
6:00–7:15	Went to Mrs. Wolf's, saw Sister Thacker and others, had religious talk and sang.
7:15–8:00	Went to Mr. Exall's for tea and religious talk.
8:00–10:30	Sang, etc. at Mr. Exall's. There was lively zeal and confession of sin.
10:30–11:30	Returned home, more religious talk and prayer.
11:30	Fell asleep.

As you can see, Wesley was no less rigorous about his religious practices after Aldersgate. If anything, he was more so! As a priest in the Church of England, he remained committed to the practices of the church.

He also remained committed to the teachings of his church. Sometimes, Christians think that having the power of God, the Holy Spirit, means that the church's rules don't matter so much. But we don't live any other area of our life like that. Having the power to drive doesn't make the rules of the road any less important for us. In fact, they become more important!

Not just that, but we come to understand the rules of the road better once we have the power to drive. Think about our remote-controlled car again. The remote-controlled car has its form, but it's lacking in power. Once it has the batteries in it, you don't take the wheels off. You drive the thing! You need the power or the car won't go. Once you have the power, you come to understand how well it was constructed in the first place. You drive it over a mound of dirt and you appreciate how the weight is distributed so it doesn't flip over. You drive it through gravel and you appreciate how the body tilts a bit to handle rough surfaces. Empowered form gets you somewhere. Power lets you see what the form is really for.

Before Georgia and before Aldersgate, one thing that set John Wesley and his friends apart at Oxford was that they took Communion, the Lord's Supper, regularly. Back then, John wrote a lesson for his students at Oxford on "the duty of constant communion." He argued that it is the responsibility of Christians to take the Lord's Supper as often as possible—at least every Sunday.

Recall that, when John went to Georgia, he got into trouble for withholding Communion from Sophia Hopkey. He was too strict about the form of godliness. Actually, "too strict" isn't the best way to say it; let's say instead that he didn't yet understand what the form of godliness was really for.

After Aldersgate, Wesley didn't change his view of the importance of Communion. Fifty-five years after he wrote his lesson at Oxford on the duty of constant Communion, John Wesley published a sermon titled "The Duty of Constant Communion." At the top, he wrote: "The following discourse was written above five and fifty years ago, for the use of my pupils at Oxford. . . . I thank God I have not yet seen cause to alter my sentiments in any point which is therein delivered. J.W."

In other words, John never changed his view of the importance of Communion. He kept the form of godliness. He held to it even more firmly once he received the power of God.

Another way John talked about the forms of godliness after Aldersgate, or what we called his "methodical" approach to faith in previous chapters, was by saying that before Aldersgate he had the faith of a servant, and after the faith of a child.

The faith of a servant is a kind of faith, maybe it is the kind of faith you have now. A servant believes she ought to obey the commands of the master. A servant knows things will go badly if she doesn't obey those commands. But the faith of a servant is incomplete faith. A servant lives in a house, but that house isn't really her home, at least not in the way it is the child's home.

The faith of a child is the real, true, full faith. A child doesn't live in fear of the master like the servant. A child knows the master's heart and understands the master's will. The master is the child's *father*! This doesn't mean the child won't obey the commands of the master. The child will follow the master's commands because the child knows those commands are safe paths to happiness. The child knows the master's commands reveal the master's heart. The child loves life in the house, even the master's rules, because the house is the child's home.

After Aldersgate, John Wesley quit being a servant in the house of God and became a child in his Father's home. God wants the same for the rest of us. He wants us to be at home.

QUESTIONS FOR DISCUSSION

1. John Wesley understood that we need both the forms of godliness and also the power of God. Right now, which one of these do you think you need God to help you with more?

2. John Wesley faithfully practiced the forms of godliness, but still needed the power of God. How do you think the power of God can help you to become more like Jesus?

3. How is your story like John Wesley's story? How are you similar to him and how are you different from him?

What Did John Wesley Do?

"My gracious Master and my God,
assist me to proclaim,
to spread thro' all the earth abroad
the honors of your name."

—Charles Wesley, "O for a Thousand Tongues"

In the last chapter, we pointed out that the power of God doesn't replace the form of godliness. It fills it. It makes it *go*. As we said, having the power to drive doesn't make the rules of the road any less important for us. In fact, they become more important!

Think about our remote-controlled car again. The car has its form, but it's lacking in power. Once it has its power, you don't take the wheels off. You drive it all around the neighborhood! You need the power or the car won't go. And once you have the power, you come to understand how well it was constructed in the first place. You drive it over a mound of dirt and it doesn't flip over. Empowered form gets you somewhere. Power lets you see what the form is really for.

But something else happens once you get power to the remote-controlled car. You come to understand what is really essential to the form and what is not. It is essential that the car has wheels, that its weight is distributed properly, and so on. It is not so essential that it has a flashy spoiler on the back. Once the power shows you what the form is for, you can see what is really essential. If you are building monster trucks, you don't need windows. If you are building race cars, you don't need back seats.

In the last lesson, we talked about how the power of home fills up the form of a house. But power does something else: it *adds* to the form. It makes changes when needed.

Let's say you move into a new house. You bring in all the things you need to live: the beds, refrigerator, and lights. But you might also need more space. When families have kids, they might need to add a new bedroom. As the family grows, they might need to knock down a wall to make the dining room bigger.

When Wesley received the power of God, he saw the importance of the forms of godliness the church had taught him. But he also understood how to design and develop new forms of godliness for the particular time and place he lived; namely, eighteenth-century England. It was these new forms, added to the classic forms, that made Methodism explode.

One of the earliest Methodists who practiced methodical faith with John and Charles Wesley at Oxford was named George Whitefield. In February 1739, nine months after John Wesley's Aldersgate experience, Whitefield began to preach to the poor out in the fields near the city of Bristol, England. People swarmed to hear him preach, and Whitefield suddenly found himself preaching to tens of thousands of people.

In England, where John Wesley developed Methodism, the country is divided into parishes. Parishes are sort of like counties for the church. Whoever lives or works in a county shares a common police force, tax code, and set of government officials who oversee the duties of the county government. Like our county officials, English parishes have their own officials who oversee the duties of the church. At the center of the parish is the church, and the priest is responsible for the faith of the parish. Among other duties, the priest decides who can preach in the pulpit of the parish church.

Whitefield's field preaching was not very popular with the priests in the parish churches. For one thing, he would just set up under a tree, in a field, in a marketplace, even a mineshaft, not in the pulpit of the parish. This practice pulled the church away from the buildings and pulpits of the parish where the priest maintained oversight. Moreover, preaching in fields and mineshafts attracted many of the most improper, untidy, and roughest members of English society. Field preaching was for people who worked in fields and labored in the mines outside of town. Field preaching was for the poor.

At first, John Wesley opposed Whitefield's field preaching. After all, these were proper Englishmen. They went to the best university in the world! More important, John saw Whitefield's field preaching as a threat to the proper forms of godliness, and a violation of the important responsibility of the parish priests to oversee the spiritual lives of the people who lived in their parishes.

But John couldn't resist the power of God for long. On April 2, 1739, less than a year after Aldersgate, Wesley preached in the fields outside Bristol for the first time, to a crowd of three or four thousand!

In one sense, George Whitefield and John Wesley's new style of preaching changed the form of Christian preaching. But, in another, it simply brought back something old that was missing. They were preaching like Jesus did; they preached out in the open to the common people.

John Wesley never looked back. A month after his first sermon in the fields he was preaching to crowds of 10,000. In another month, 15,000. By September, his crowds in and around London grew to 20,000. Meanwhile, Whitefield's crowds swelled to 30,000! 2

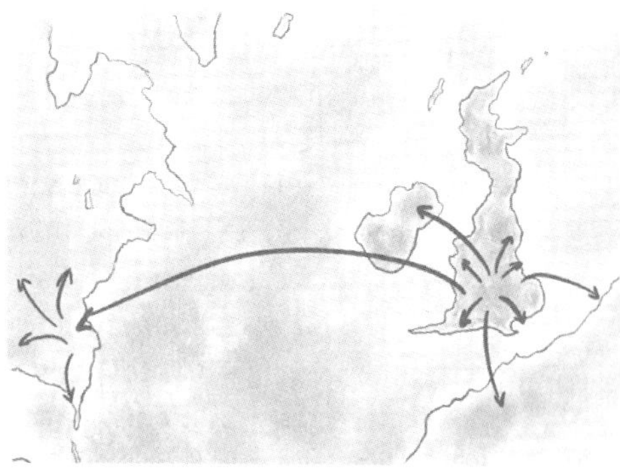

A revival was sweeping across England, and Wesley and Whitefield were feeding it. Wesley never tired. By the end of his life, John Wesley had preached more than 42,000 sermons.

Now, imagine you are John Wesley. You have been preaching to tens of thousands in the fields and marketplaces of England. Everywhere you go, people are wanting to know more about the power of God. They want to know how to pursue it. What would you do?

As remarkable as the sermons and crowds were, what really set John Wesley apart was his ability to organize all these people in the pursuit of God. In fact, he handled this responsibility so well that, by the time John Wesley died, the movement that began with the small group of Methodist Bible Moths at Oxford had gathered more than 70,000 people in Britain and 60,000 in America! 3

The key to Wesley's success was his ability to bring the people he reached through field preaching into a serious, methodical pursuit of the Christian life. Wesley saw that the people who heard his preaching needed something the church wasn't providing. They needed to pursue the fullness of the gospel by being reshaped in the Christian community.

LISTENING
CROWDS

SOCIETIES

CLASSES

BANDS

To meet this need, Wesley developed a series of groups, carefully structured to draw people closer and closer to God. Picture a funnel. At the widest level, where the greatest amount of fluid can fit, are the crowds of people who gathered around Wesley in the fields and marketplaces of England. They listened, learned a bit, and some of them felt the call of God to deepen their faith. A bit lower down the funnel would be those who felt that call to deepened faith. They gathered in Societies each week to read Scripture, pray, sing spiritual songs, and encourage one another. They also met in Classes where they would ask one another every week, "How is it with your soul? Where have you met Christ this week?" Finally, at the bottom of the funnel were those who wanted the deepest faith. Each week they met in Bands, where they confessed all their sins to a small group of other Christians. 

John Wesley's preaching and organization of Methodists into Societies, Classes, and Bands was so successful that the movement boomed. He quickly realized the leaders and members of the Methodist movement needed teaching and guidance on a large scale. So somehow, while traveling more than 250,000 miles in carriages and on horseback (that would be ten trips around the globe!), preaching 42,000 sermons, and managing the Societies and Classes, Wesley also managed to publish more than five hundred books, tracts, and magazines! Add to that about nine thousand hymns written by Charles Wesley (ever sing "Hark the Herald Angels Sing" at Christmas?), and the Wesleys were some of the most productive writers of the eighteenth century.

John's published works are sprawling. Of the many sermons he wrote and delivered, he published about 150 of them, all carefully crafted to teach Methodists and help preachers learn and teach the faith. He published notes on the entire Bible, including his own personal translations of the original Greek of the New Testament. Remarkably, he edited fifty books for what he called *A Christian Library*. These books are filled with selections from Christian writers throughout the history of Christianity—from the apostles to his contemporaries. He wrote and published books about how to change your voice and move your arms when preaching sermons. He often wrote and published tracts, or short booklets, on major topics in Christian theology. ✳

But Wesley's writing wasn't only for the leaders of the Methodists. He also wrote for ordinary people. He published books on English, French, Greek, and Hebrew grammar. He published works in philosophy and medicine. He published popular magazines with tips for prayer and for good hygiene. In short, he offered all Methodists not only spiritual guidance but attempted to provide for their general education. As the Methodists grew, they were sometimes harassed by other groups in England. Remember, a lot of the early Methodists were not the most respectable English folks. So he published tracts defending the Methodists and explaining their practices.

In this way, too, John Wesley and George Whitefield were like Jesus. With His preaching and healing and love for people on the edges, Jesus attracted criticism from those who thought that the forms of religion could never be expanded.

Wesley's commitment to forms of godliness empowered by the power of God led him to work tirelessly for the Christian faith. This effort, enabled by the power of God, changed the shape of not only England, but world Christianity forever.

QUESTIONS FOR DISCUSSION

1. John Wesley understood the importance of community in helping us to live like Jesus. What groups are you a part of that help you to live a Christian life? What more do you need to do to be more "methodical" about your spiritual growth?

2. John Wesley and George Whitefield's preaching brought thousands to Christ. In what ways are you spreading the good news to those who need to hear it?

3. As we see in John Wesley's life and ministry, the power of God changes things when it is present. How can the power of God change the way you live?

UNIT 2:

WHAT DID WESLEY TEACH?

LESSON 5

What Is the Goal of the Christian Life?

As we said in the last lesson, Wesley's preaching and movement drew in thousands and thousands of people almost immediately. But what was Wesley preaching that attracted so many? We can sum it up in two words: *go further*. God wants you to go further. God has been working since the beginning of time so that you can go further.

But if you want to go somewhere you've never been before you need a reliable guide. You want someone who has made the journey and knows the way.

Let's say you want to get to Alaska. You go to the bus station and you ask the driver, "Is this bus headed to Alaska?" The driver answers, "Maybe so. Who knows?"

Would you get on the bus or would you look for another bus with a better driver?

If you are wise, you would grab your bags and look for another bus.

Big goals require guides. This is as true for traveling as it is for learning to play the piano. If you showed up for piano lessons, and your teacher handed you a basketball to dribble, you would probably ask what that has to do with learning the piano. If the teacher responded, "Well, how should I know? Perhaps it will!" you would be wise to put the ball down and find another piano teacher.

Every important goal needs good guidance. Want to go to Alaska? You need a driver who doesn't need to ask for directions. Want to play piano? You need a teacher who knows the difference between the melody line and a free-throw line. Want to climb Mount Everest? You need a sherpa. Want to be like Jesus? You need wise, mature Christians.

What makes a reliable guide? First of all, they need to know the destination. Second, they need to know how to get there.

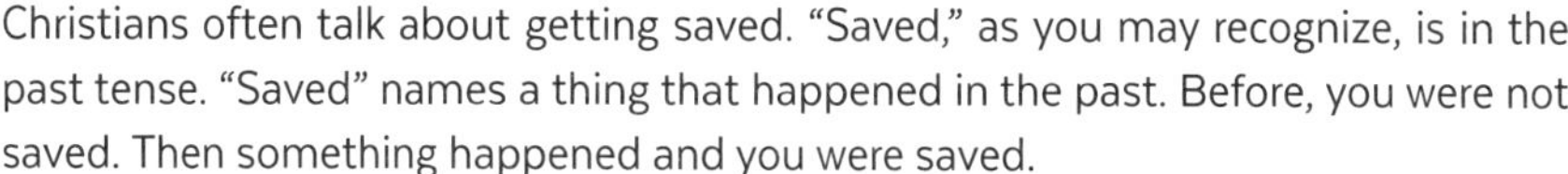

John Wesley's preaching worked because he knew the goal. John Wesley's movement grew because he knew how to get there. What was the goal?

Christians often talk about getting saved. "Saved," as you may recognize, is in the past tense. "Saved" names a thing that happened in the past. Before, you were not saved. Then something happened and you were saved.

We often associate being saved with a moment of prayer, like when you asked Jesus to come into your heart. This is true enough, as far as it goes. But it isn't the whole story.

In Acts 9, a sinner named Saul was traveling down the road, just after holding coats while his friends stoned a Christian to death. He was as far from being Christian as you could imagine. Then he encountered Christ and the goal of his life was totally changed. He stopped persecuting Christians. He became a Christian. He even started calling himself by a different name, Paul, and telling other people about Jesus. He was saved from his old life. But God wasn't done with Paul. God kept working in Paul to make him more and more like Jesus. God wanted him to go further.

That same Paul prays in the letter to the Ephesians "that Christ may dwell in your hearts through faith, *as you are being rooted and grounded in love*" (Eph. 3:17, emphasis added). You see, when you ask Jesus to come into your heart, He does. He changes the goal of your life. But then He really gets to work—He starts rooting and grounding you in love. ✸

In another letter, Paul writes, "I am confident of this, that the one who began a good work among you will bring it to completion by the day of Jesus Christ" (Phil. 1:6). Through faith we are saved (Eph. 2:8-9). God begins a good work in us. He gives us a new goal, but Christ continues to work in us until we reach that goal. He's not content until our sin is completely defeated.

Salvation is that whole work of Christ, from start to finish. Christ wants to set you free from sin. He wants you to *go further*.

Most of the time, when Wesley thought about salvation, he thought about the *whole* of that work—the critical moment when Christ *enters* the heart, and also the work He *continues* to do once He gets there.

For Wesley, salvation names the beginning, whether in a moment of prayer or in our baptism as infants. It names the continued work of setting us free from sin;

and, it turns out, being set free from sin takes a lot of work.

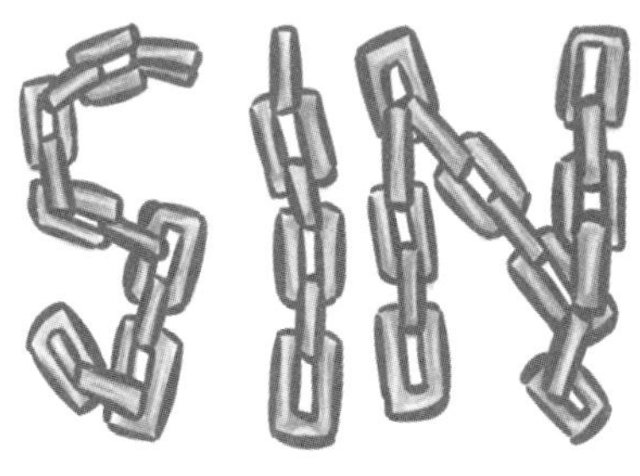

But being set free from sin isn't the end of the story. God still wants us to go further. Christ wants to set us free *from sin,* but He also wants to set us free *for something.*

Anyone who has been in time-out, or in detention, or in jail, knows how hard it is, even for a few minutes, to be stuck where you don't want to be. When you're a kid in time-out, you can't wait to be free. When you're a student in detention, the minutes drag; the clock seems to move slower than usual. Prisoners count the days until their release. All of us long to be free. But when you get out of detention you'll wind up there again if you don't know what the purpose of school really is. Unless you understand that school is for learning, you won't do your homework, you won't pay attention in class, and you won't listen to the teachers—these are precisely the sorts of things that get you into trouble. Unless you learn what freedom is *for,* you'll just abuse your freedom *again.* You might try harder not to get caught, but you'll probably end up back in detention before long.

What does Christ want to set us free for? Wesley summed it up in a word: *holiness.* What is holiness? When we say a thing is holy, we sometimes think of it like it's something too special to touch or get close to. But holiness, most basically, is the character of God. We talk about the Holy Spirit. When we say some things are holy, this is not because they need to be kept away from us, but because they have come close to God. God likes to come close to things. Jesus shows us this. When God comes close to things, the holiness of God rubs off on them. They become like God. Being holy, then, is becoming like God.

Freedom from sin for holiness—this is the whole work of God. That's how far God wants to take us. This is our final goal.

Wesley kept that goal at the center of all his work. He studied, carefully, how God moves the Christian toward the goal of freedom from sin for holiness. Wesley loved to have spiritual conversations with holy people, those whose lives looked like Christ's. He interviewed them. He studied their faith and habits. He thought hard about the ways Christ works in the hearts where He has made His home. And, over time, Wesley became a reliable guide.

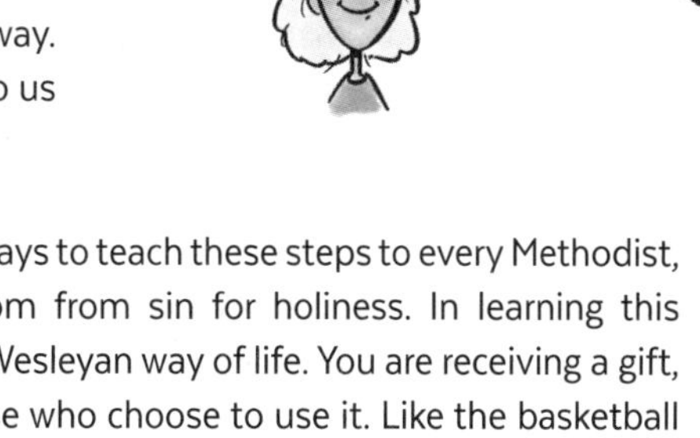

As a guide, he developed a clear sequence of steps for those of us on the path to freedom from sin for holiness. That sequence of steps is the heart of Methodism. Methodists are the ones who follow that Wesleyan way. They follow the method handed down to us from John Wesley.

Over time, Methodists have developed ways to teach these steps to every Methodist, to help them along the way to freedom from sin for holiness. In learning this sequence of steps, you are learning the Wesleyan way of life. You are receiving a gift, one that has been proven useful to those who choose to use it. Like the basketball coach teaches his players how to shoot, Wesleyans teach young Christians this way of life. And so, in learning this sequence of steps, you will carry with you the heart of our tradition.

We have been calling this a "sequence of steps." There are two important ideas in that phrase: (1) a sequence, and (2) steps. Let's start with the second.

Steps make us think of travel. Now, imagine you are going to make a journey of a thousand miles on foot. Let's assume the average person's step is around two or so feet. A mile is 5,280 feet, and so the average person can walk a mile in about 2,640 steps. Multiply that by a thousand, and a journey of a thousand miles turns out to be about 2,640,000 steps.

But that is just if you are only concerned to make a thousand-mile journey, and you don't care where it takes you. In that case, you could take 2,640,000 steps in your living room, and finish by collapsing on the same couch where you started. But that doesn't sound like a lot of fun. We would be pretty upset if we spent all that energy

and never saw anything but the four walls of our living room. If I set out from my living room on a journey of 2,640,000 steps, I could be in Miami or Dallas. What a wasted opportunity to march around my living room!

The same goes for our spiritual life. We need to take steps, but we need to take them toward somewhere. We need the steps lined up in a direction. They need to be put in sequence. Methodists sometimes talk about the Wesleyan way of salvation. We sometimes make it sound fancy with Latin, calling it the *via salutis*. *Via salutis* just means "way of salvation." A *via salutis*, or way of salvation, is just the sequence of steps we take in our journey to freedom from sin for holiness.

On the way to freedom from sin for holiness, we need the right sequence of steps. And John Wesley proved to be a reliable guide in finding the right sequence of steps. The next four lessons will introduce you to that sequence of steps, the Wesleyan way.

QUESTIONS FOR DISCUSSION

1. What is the goal of the Christian life? Are you moving toward this goal?

2. Why is a method so important for us as Christians?

3. How does John Wesley help us to understand what the Bible means by "salvation"?

What Is Repentance?

> "Now incline me to repent!
> Let me now my fall lament!
> Now my foul revolt deplore!
> Weep, believe, and sin no more."
>
> —Charles Wesley, "Depth of Mercy"

In the last lesson, we said that Wesley knew God's goal for us: to set us free from sin for holiness.

As we said, this work is definitely about setting us free from sin. In fact, God wants to set us totally and completely free from the power of sin. One of the most famous hymns written by Charles Wesley is called "O for a Thousand Tongues to Sing." Perhaps you have sung it in your church. The original hymn had nineteen verses! Here's the fourth:

> He breaks the power of canceled sin,
> He sets the prisoner free;
> His blood can make the foulest clean,
> His blood availed for me.

"He breaks the power of canceled sin, He sets the prisoner free." In those two little lines, Charles summarizes a key teaching of the Wesleyan way: it's possible to be really, truly free from sin.

Getting free from sin isn't easy though. Breaking us free from the power of sin is a big job. Sin is strong, like a bear trap; it's tricky to escape, like a maze.

This is why a key step in saving us from sin is *repentance*. Repentance means a change of life. When we repent, we recognize that the way we've been going isn't the right way. This involves the heart, but it also involves the mind. This is why the Greek word for repentance is *metanoia,* which literally means a "change of mind."

We need to be *healed* from sin, but we need to *see* our sin first.

Imagine you were born with blurry vision, on an island of people with blurry vision. No one ever tells you clear vision is possible. No one you know has ever seen clearly. No one makes eyeglasses, because no one thinks to improve their vision. Everyone draws in huge images so people can make them out. Everyone designs things that appeal to blurry vision. Everyone writes in a large, dark script. In fact, your language doesn't even have a word for "clear" or for "blurry" with regard to sight. You just see. Well, sort of.

If you lived on the Island of Blurry Vision, it would never occur to you that you have a problem. As far as you know, human beings just have blurry vision. It would never occur to you that your vision could be otherwise, that clarity is something you want in your vision.

Do you have a problem? Of course! Playing baseball on the Island of Blurry Vision would be painful. But you actually have two problems. First, you can't see well, which is a serious hassle. But second, and most important, you don't even know that you can't see well. You are blind to the problem of blurry vision!

Sin is a similar kind of double problem, only worse.

Sin is a problem in the first way: you are sick with sin.

And sin is a problem in the second way: it's a problem you don't even know you have. Everyone else has it too! Indeed, unless God told us, we wouldn't have any idea.

But sin is also a problem in a third way. The more you sin, the *less* you are aware of it. The more you sin, the more likely you are to deny the idea that you are a sinner. If an optometrist showed up and started making glasses on the Island of Blurry Vision, there would be a mad rush! But when we're told we're full of sin, we usually don't want to listen. In fact, there is usually a mad rush *away* from the person telling us we're sinful! This is a bit like avoiding going to the doctor because the doctor always tells us we have a problem. Sin makes us hide from the truth, so we become more and more sinful.

Let's say you're taking a history class and you have a big paper due. You should have been working on it, but you've been putting off the reading. Your mom asks you, "How's the paper going?" You say it's going fine. The assignment is starting to stress you out, so you go play a video game instead. Your dad asks, "Did you finish the paper?" You know you shouldn't be playing video games before you finish your paper, so you lie and say, "Yep." Later on, you try and go to your room and close the door to finish the paper. Then you realize you need a book from the library, and you can't drive. Uh oh. If you don't say anything, you can't finish the paper, but if you ask your parents for a ride to the library, they'll know you lied to them. A little lie to your mom that everything was fine turned into a bigger lie to your dad that you were done with the paper. Now you have a problem with the paper and with your parents.

Sin is like this. Little sins lead to bigger ones. And sin leads us further away from the only Source of help. When we try and dig ourselves out of the hole, it only gets deeper. Sin is like a snowball rolling down a hill—it gets bigger as it goes.

Every time you sin, it gets easier to sin more, and then it gets even easier, until sinning becomes second nature. It becomes what you do automatically.

When you get away with sin, the only thing you get away from is God. When you lie to God, you lie to yourself. You break off your relationship to God, and so you break yourself off from the only one that can heal you from the sickness of sin. You become blind to your blindness.

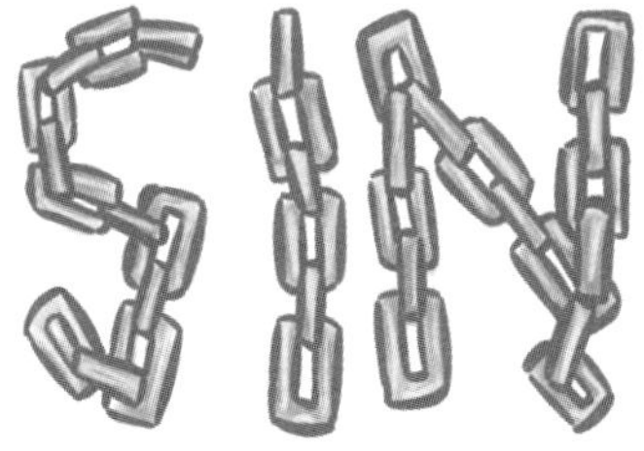

Sin, then, is a threefold problem. First, there is the sin itself. Then there is the ignorance that follows. Finally, there is the way ignorance leads to more and more sin, until it becomes automatic. Sinning is a wicked cycle. This is the power of sin that Charles Wesley talked about. It's this wicked cycle that Jesus came to break, to set us prisoners free from its power.

"He breaks the power of canceled sin, He sets the prisoner free." The Wesleyan way is clear on this: we don't only need to have our sins canceled. Of course, we need our sins canceled, but we don't just need our sin canceled. If the first problem gets wiped away, we still have the other two problems. We have become ignorant of how deep our sin has become, so deep that it has become second nature—automatic. So, along with (1) having our sin canceled and forgiven, we also (2) need the power of that sin broken. Only when sin is canceled and its power is broken will we be truly free.

So how does God cancel sin and break its power?

When the optometrist sends a letter to the Island of Blurry Vision, it does no good. It's hard to explain clear vision to people who don't even know what blurry vision is. So what is the optometrist to do? The optometrist needs to set sail.

Imagine the optometrist is so concerned about the inhabitants of the Island of Blurry Vision that he braves the journey. He shows up with his instruments prepared to administer eye exams, craft lenses, and hand out a couple thousand pairs of glasses.

Now, imagine you happen to be on the shoreline as the optometrist arrives. He pulls out a chair, waves some cards around, and calls out: "You think you can see, but you have never seen clearly. Just have a seat and I'll show you what it means to really see!"

What would you do?

Unless someone sits in the chair and follows his instructions, no one will ever learn the difference between clear and blurry vision. Unless someone submits to the optometrist, submits to the laws and practices of optometry, baseball will never have a chance on the Island of Blurry Vision.

But as soon as someone sits, looks where the optometrist says to look, and lets him hold the lenses to their eyes, everything changes on the Island of Blurry Vision.

As you have probably figured out, the optometrist who makes the journey to the Island of Blurry Vision is a lot like the Son, who makes the journey to us in Jesus Christ. Just like the optometrist, Jesus came to teach us that something has gone wrong. He came to tell us that we have a big problem: sin. It was a problem He could see and name because He knew life could be lived without it. He knew life was meant to be lived without it. And because He is God, Jesus has the power and knowledge to fix the problem.

But we have to submit. Optometrists can't fix our eyes unless we sit in their chair, look through their lenses, and answer their questions. You have to submit to them; it is the same with God.

Repentance is a lot like submitting to the optometrist. It's admitting we are ignorant, and submitting to the one who knows. It's admitting that we have become stuck in sin—that we sin automatically—and submitting to the one who lives without sin. Repentance isn't work, but giving up on our way of working, because our way of working has gone wrong. It's giving up on our way of working so God can work on us. So God can work *in* us.

The Wesleyan way is a way of repentance, but a way of repentance is a way in a funny sense. It is a way in the sense that it has a destination. It has a goal: freedom from sin for holiness. But it's not like a lot of other paths, in the sense that you can make it on your own strength. Rather, repentance is learning to admit your weakness. It's learning to let yourself be helped. The way up the mountain is long and steep. We can't do it on our own. Only by letting the expert mountain climber help us can we get up the mountain at all. Saint Paul says this best when he writes that God's strength is made perfect in our weakness (2 Cor. 12:9).

For the sick person, the first step in being healed is to admit to the doctor that she is sick.

For someone with blurry vision, the first step in seeing well is to admit that he needs glasses.

For the student who is hopelessly behind on his project, the first step is to admit he needs help. He needs a ride to the library.

For the prisoner, the first step to being freed is to admit that he's locked in chains.

The good news is that God is ready and able to help us. His strength is made perfect in our weakness.

QUESTIONS FOR DISCUSSION

1. Have you ever suffered from low expectations? How do lowered expectations prevent us from the fullness of Christian life?

2. What is repentance? How does repentance help to make us more like Jesus? Can you think of a specific time that you had to repent—to change your mind and change your direction?

3. How does sin blind us to the truth and cause us to get stuck? Can you think of a specific example?

What Is Justification and New Birth?

"My chains fell off, my heart was free;
I rose, went forth and followed Thee."

—Charles Wesley, "And Can It Be, That I Should Gain"

What does God do when we submit to Him? What does God do when we repent? This lesson and the next will talk about this in two ways.

First, in this lesson, we're going to talk about what God does in us. We'll explain how God *operates* on our sin, so that it's canceled and gone. Second, in the next lesson, we're going to talk about what God does with us from that point forward. We'll explain how God *cooperates* with us so that the power of sin is broken and we are totally free.

Every journey has a start. You start a marathon with a first step. No step, no marathon. The same is true of our journey on the Wesleyan way of salvation. No step, no salvation. But what is that first step on this journey? And who takes it?

The second question is easier to answer: only God can save. Remember how bad our problem of sin is—it's like you have blurry vision, you don't know it, and it's getting worse. There's nothing you can do to heal the problem of sin. You need God to take care of it. So God needs to act on your behalf. God needs to set us on the way to holiness. God takes the first step.

Christians have talked about this first step in several ways. John Wesley, when he explained the Wesleyan way, usually talked about two things God does when He sets us on the way to holiness: God offers us *justification* and *new birth*.

Although justification and new birth are two different ideas, they always happen at the same moment. It's kind of like getting married. When you get married, two different things happen at the same moment. First, you form a new relationship. You are now a spouse. Second, something totally new comes about. There is now a family. Justification and new birth are kind of like this. We can talk about what happens in this decisive moment when God acts in two different ways, but they hang together like the relationship between two spouses and a family. If you don't have one, you don't get the other. If you have one, you get the other.

So what are justification and new birth? John Wesley, in a famous sermon entitled "The Scripture Way of Salvation," says this: "And at the same time that we are justified, yea, in that very moment . . . we are 'born again,' 'born from above,' 'born of the Spirit.' There is a *real* as well as a *relative* change."

"A *real* as well as a *relative* change." Justification, Wesley says, is a relative change. It is a change in the relationship between us and God. It's forgiveness. New birth is a real change. It is a change, not in our relationship, but in ourselves. We are really changed. What could this mean?

Imagine a vampire named Drake. Drake skulks about after dark, capturing unsuspecting victims. He's done this for centuries; they don't call vampires "the undead" for nothing.

One night, as he strolls through the forest, Drake happens upon a man who has foolishly wandered out alone. Drake's hungry, so he does what vampires do. As he walks back home for a long day's rest, Drake passes a small hut at the edge of the forest, and there a small girl sits waiting anxiously. "Papa," she calls. Suddenly, it hits him: he killed her father. For the first time in his vampiric life, Drake feels remorse. He thinks of all the children who might go hungry, robbed of their parents by his appetites. He sheds a tear, and decides he will try to make it up to this child.

Now, imagine that Drake leaves packages of food and money every day for the next ten years. Then, after the child is grown, he encounters her in the forest one evening on a similar stroll to her father's home. Drake fights down his impulses, and gathers the strength to confess and apologize. He explains everything: his murder and his sorrow and his remorse and his gifts. Imagine, by some miracle, she finds the courage to forgive him. Just like that, the relationship changes. Drake is no longer her debtor. He is forgiven. He has been set free from the bondage of the past ten years. There is a relational change.

But there is still a problem. *Drake is still a vampire!* He still has the desire, and the need, for blood. And no matter how earnest this girl's forgiveness, Drake remains the same kind of thing that needs to drink blood for life. There is a relational change, but not a real change. Drake is forgiven, but he's still a monster.

Or think about it like this. A prisoner is released from a long prison sentence. Upon release, he finds himself poor, hungry, and without any options. A priest gives him a meal and a bed for the night. During dinner, the prisoner sees the priest's fine silver in the dining room. He thinks, *If only I had a bit of that silver, I could find a place to stay*

and figure out what I should do next. So later that evening, he rises, steals a few select pieces of silverware and sneaks off into the night.

The next afternoon, a policeman happens upon the prisoner sleeping on the street. He discovers the silverware with the priest's initials on them, so the policeman carries the prisoner back to the priest for an explanation. Now the priest, to the prisoner's surprise, greets him as a friend. He scolds the prisoner for his forgetfulness. The priest brings out the rest of the silver and then goes back for several fine, rather large pieces of jewelry and gold. He gives them to the prisoner. He tells him not to be so forgetful as he sets out on his new path in life. And then he releases him, to the policeman's great surprise.

In this case, two changes take place. First, there is a change of *relationship*. The priest changes the prisoner from a thief into a friend; he gives him gifts. Second, there is a *real* change. The prisoner is given a new life. His financial worries are over, and now he can pursue the new life that suits him. What was impossible before has become possible. There is both a relational and a real change.

Justification is the relational change. What is changed is our relationship to God. We were once lost; now we are found. We were once enemies of God; now we are friends. We were once guilty; now we are pardoned. God has acted to completely obliterate the relationship we once had with Him. We are forgiven. We are washed clean of the stain of sin. We are saved (Rom. 5:1–11).

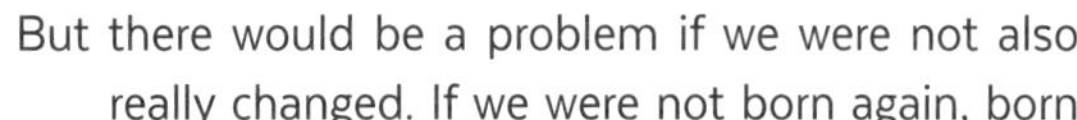

But there would be a problem if we were not also really changed. If we were not born again, born anew, we would be like Drake the vampire, forgiven but plagued by desires we are powerless to overcome. We need God to both change our relationship and to change us. We need a real change. That real change is what Wesley called the "new birth."

When Jesus taught us about the new birth in John 3, He said some funny things. "No one can enter the kingdom of God without being born of water and Spirit. What is born of the flesh is flesh, and what is born of the Spirit is spirit" (vv. 5–6). It's a bizarre teaching. But it's an essential teaching. We must be born of the Spirit. The new birth is sort of like the prisoner set on his way with the priest's gold and silver. Not only has his relationship changed, from thief to friend, but now he has the resources to set out on a totally new, totally different path of life.

But the new birth is even better. The gift we are given is not just some valuable good, like gold or silver. We receive God Himself. The Holy Spirit comes and dwells in us. The Spirit of Christ makes a home in us. God doesn't give us anything less than God. So, Jesus says, we are "born of the Spirit." That is how God makes us new.

Now pause and think about that for a minute.

Imagine the girl takes Drake under the cover of night to the house of a holy man who gives him a blessed potion to drink. The potion burns as Drake drinks it down. It doesn't taste good, like blood usually does. Every cell in his body feels like it's about to explode. He thinks he's about to die. But then he takes another sip, and it tastes different. Now the potion is delicious. Suddenly, he feels something he hasn't felt in a long time. He feels alive. As the night passes and the sun rises, Drake enjoys the feeling of the sun on his face. He has a new life now. A life in the sun, with other people, free from the thirst for blood.

This might seem like a silly analogy, but it's not too far from the image used by Paul in Ephesians 2. Paul writes that we "were dead through [our] trespasses and sins," but God made us "alive together with Christ" (vv. 1–5).

This is what follows after repentance. We are justified; we are given a restored relationship with God. And we are reborn; we are given a new life.

QUESTIONS FOR DISCUSSION

1. What is the difference between justification and new birth? Have you experienced these in your life?

2. How does John Wesley help us to understand the process of salvation? What are the steps Wesley has taught us so far?

3. In the analogy from the chapter, have you ever felt like the vampire? Have you ever felt like you know your sin hurts people, but have been unable to change?

What Is Sanctification?

> "A charge to keep I have,
> A God to glorify,
> A never-dying soul to save,
> And fit it for the sky."
>
> —Charles Wesley, "A Charge to Keep I Have"

In the last lesson, we talked about how God *operates on us* in justification and new birth. In this chapter, we want to talk about how God *cooperates with us*, after justification and new birth, to lead us toward holiness.

What does it mean for us to cooperate with God? Imagine your neighbor is really good at playing the upright bass. You sit and listen, and marvel at the speed of her fingers, her ability to make your feet tap with the slap of her hands, and the smooth, deep sounds she conjures from the giant strings. You sit and listen, and you wonder what it would be like to play like that. But you could never play like that, because you don't have an upright bass. You don't even know where to buy one. And even if, by some miracle, you had one, how would you learn how to play it? So you're stuck listening and wondering.

Now imagine your neighbor gave you an upright bass, and then gave you free lessons. And over time, by listening to her instruction, and practicing the drills she taught you, you learn to play, not exactly like her, but in your own way that is just as good.

If you were prideful, you might think you had done this on your own. But you didn't. When you started you were utterly, totally bass-less. If she hadn't given you the gift of an upright bass and then taught you how to use it, you would still be stuck listening and wondering.

It's kind of like this when God leads us toward holiness. We might think we're doing a lot of work. But really, we wouldn't be able to do anything if God didn't act first. No free gift of an upright bass, no playing the bass. No new birth, no holiness. Moreover, we wouldn't know what to do with the bass if we didn't have a teacher. Likewise, we wouldn't know what to do with the new birth if God didn't show us. No teacher, no playing the bass. No Guide, no holiness.

But the new birth is different than the upright bass in an important way. As we said in the last chapter, the new birth is the gift of God Himself. The Holy Spirit resides in us. So really, it's kind of like God cooperates with God. We get pulled along for the ride!

This is not surprising if we understand what holiness, or sanctification, actually is.

One of Jesus' disciples, Peter, wrote a letter to a group of early churches that were being persecuted for their faith. In this letter he instructs the Christians: "as he who called you is holy, be holy yourselves in all your conduct; for it is written, 'You shall be holy, for I am holy'" (1 Peter 1:15–16).

God's plan for us has always been to make us holy, to set us apart. When Peter says, "be holy," he is quoting Leviticus 11 where God tells the Israelites the kinds of animals they should or should not eat. It's kind of an odd idea, but God wants to make us so distinct, so set apart, so holy, that our connection to God shapes all of our decisions. Who you date. Where you study. Even what you order for lunch. ✸

The key point here is that God calls His people to be different. Different from the world and different from the way we were when God first saved us. The way God makes us different is by sharing His own holiness with us.

In both the Old and New Testaments, we see that God wants the same thing: that we would be holy, just as God is holy. God wants us to become like God. Peter wrote a second letter to the persecuted Christians, and he returns to this idea. He says that Christ came so that we could "become participants of the divine nature" (2 Peter 1:3–4). Jesus gives us everything we need—justification and new birth—so that we can live a godly, or holy, life. So that we can be set apart. 

This idea is everywhere in Scripture. Paul tells us to be like Jesus. Since Jesus is God, "be like Jesus" means "be like God." So Paul says, "until Christ is formed in you" (Gal. 4:19).

John Wesley loved to talk about this idea. He loved to preach about sanctification. *Sanctification* is a big word, but it's a pretty straightforward idea. To be sanctified is to be holy like God. The saints are people who show us God, who live like Christ, who live like God.

Sanctification is the twofold process of *dying to sin* and *growing in grace.* ✸

Now, most of us realize that we have problems. We need to die to sin. We look at our embarrassing sins and bad habits and wish that we could be rid of them. We want God to remove the things that pain us, like a surgeon cutting out cancer or stitching up a wound. It's easy to imagine dying to sin. But growing in grace can be harder to envision, like a bird that has never flown might have a hard time imagining what it's like to soar among the clouds.

C. S. Lewis paints a powerful picture of sanctification in his book, *Mere Christianity*:

Imagine yourself as a living house. God comes in to rebuild that house. At first, perhaps, you can understand what He is doing. He is getting the drains right and stopping the leaks in the roof and so on; you knew that those jobs needed doing and so you are not surprised. But presently he starts knocking the house about in a way that hurts abominably and does not seem to make sense. What on earth is He up to? The explanation is that He is building quite a different house from the one you thought of—throwing out a new wing here, putting on an extra floor there, running up towers, making courtyards. You thought you were going to be made into a decent little cottage; but He is building a palace. He intends to come and live in it Himself.

What God wants to do for us isn't just to pick us up, dust us off a bit, and set us back on our way. God wants to transform us, to make a real change in us, so that we can come to be like Him. So even after God gives us the gifts of justification and new birth, He doesn't stop there. We continue to be reshaped into the likeness of Christ. We continue to become like God.

We have a purpose. But it's not just to be a good-enough human being, it's to become like Jesus. We'll talk about this even more in the next lesson.

QUESTIONS FOR DISCUSSION

1. What is sanctification? Is there an area of your life where you've felt God sanctifying you?

2. How do we cooperate with God in the process of sanctification?

3. Think about John Wesley's story. How did God work to sanctify him?

LESSON 9

What Is Entire Sanctification?

How holy does God want us to become? Can we really be like Jesus? Is that even possible?

Imagine you live in a small village on the edge of a forest. Your village has one road, leading two directions. Away from the forest, the road leads to the town where you trade goods, though the exchange is always bad. It's your only option for tools and housewares, so you use it, but you know you are getting ripped off.

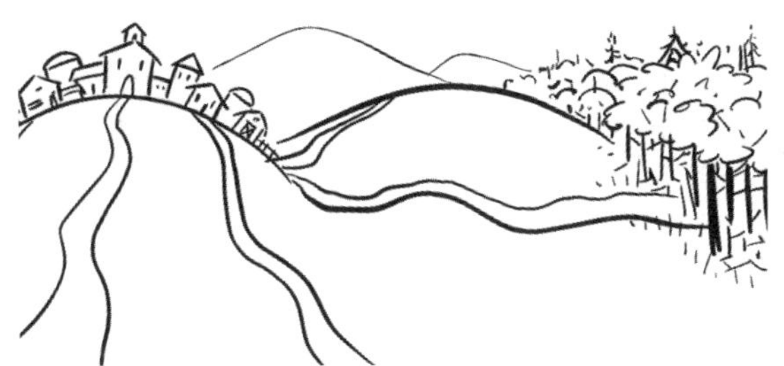

In the other direction, the road leads into the forest. No one who goes down that road ever comes back. Your village has a sort of unspoken agreement never to speak of those who wander down the forest road. As a child, you are taught it is dangerous, that thieves and murderers and monsters lie in wait to capture, torture, and kill those who travel down it.

So long as you believe those stories, you are a fool to travel down that road. And, of course, most people believe them. But every now and then someone disappears from the village. No one talks about it—there is no funeral, no memorial, nothing. Just an empty seat at the table.

The stories suggest the road is bad news. But what if the stories are wrong? What if the reason people don't come back is because they've gone somewhere wonderful? What if the road leads to Oz? Or to Narnia? Or to heaven?

Low expectations lower possibilities. Imagine thinking the only song anyone could play on the piano is "Mary Had a Little Lamb." Why bother learning the piano? Why learn to read sheet music? Why study diatonic scales? It only makes sense not to bother with it. But, of course, your belief is absurd. And it's not the piano, or the sheet music, or the diatonic scale that is to blame for it. It's your mistaken belief that has led you to low expectations from such things as pianos. 

John Wesley had high expectations about the power of God's grace. Wesley was convinced that the way of salvation leads somewhere beyond what you could ever ask or imagine. He was convinced that the way of salvation *actually* leads us to become more and more like Christ—it leads to holiness.

Now some people might say holiness is impossible. Some Christians reject the idea that we can make it very far down this road to holiness. "Sure," they say, "we are justified and born again. But from that point on we are constantly falling down and just limping along, and God is constantly forgiving our stumbles." To them, holy living is unrealistic.

But think about the holiest people you know. Not just the people who do churchy things, but people who have astonishing patience, immense love, willingness to sacrifice for the good of others. If you don't know anyone like this, think of people you have heard of, like Mother Teresa, or Billy Graham, or John Wesley. There really do seem to be saints living among us. These holy people help us to realize the possibilities for life are greater than we expected.

For Wesley, the German Moravians on the ship at sea opened his eyes to greater possibilities. When the ship almost capsized, killing them all, they had an inexplicable peace. Terrified Wesley didn't know that was possible. He never expected it. But when Wesley saw these people, he was convinced that the way of salvation leads somewhere astounding. He was convinced that there was more.

How much more? How far can we go? How holy can we be? Can we *actually* be like Christ in this life? Wesley thought so. He taught what we call "entire sanctification," or "Christian perfection." This idea is key to the Wesleyan way.

Now, *perfection* is kind of a nasty word in our world. We think being a perfectionist is a problem. We complain about "little Miss Perfect." No one wants to be that person.

But Jesus commands us: "Be perfect, therefore, as your heavenly Father is perfect" (Matt. 5:48). Of course, Jesus didn't mean that we should be a know-it-all, that we should enjoy making others feel bad because we are good, or that we should be devastated if we aren't the best at everything we try.

What, then, is Christian perfection?

Imagine someone serving you the perfect meal. Everything is just right. Every dish is delicious, and every dish complements the others. But, most important, somehow every dish is served in the perfect amount. There's  just enough to enjoy, to be pleasantly full, and then to be satisfied without that feeling of overeating.

With a meal, perfection isn't only found in exceptional quality. You also need the perfect quantity. Too much of a good thing becomes a bad thing. A perfect meal is perfectly satisfying. It makes your hunger come to a perfect end. Your appetite rests, and you are happy.

Christian perfection is kind of like this perfect end to a perfect meal. It's when your desires come to rest wholly in God, and you are truly happy. Most of our life, we are running around looking for this and that to make us truly happy. We give God some of our time, and some of our heart, but we are pulled here and there by our love for other things. Those who are perfected in Christ have come to rest in the love of God. They rest in the love of God, and so they have peace, joy, and true happiness, no matter what happens to them. They have come to rest; they love God and love others perfectly.

The entirely sanctified have true happiness, no matter what happens to them. But Christian perfection doesn't mean *life* will be perfect. Just before Jesus told us, "be perfect," He told us that His idea of happiness is different than the kind of pleasure we usually think of when we talk about being happy. It's not like the pleasure we get from a new car, or new clothes, or even the perfect meal we just talked about. Here's why: that pleasure goes away quickly, and usually is replaced by more hunger, more restlessness. Jesus' happiness is in-spite-of happiness. "Blessed are the poor in spirit," Jesus says (Matt. 5:3).

You can be poor, even poor in spirit, and be blessed, or happy. You can face death with perfect peace. Now that's a happiness worth seeking after!

Christian perfection doesn't mean life will be perfect. It also doesn't mean that you won't make mistakes. You still may not know calculus, or how to get those weird, English I's and E's in the right order. You can still catch a cold or develop cancer. You still feel hunger. And you still face temptation. After all, Jesus was tempted! But in all these difficulties, those who have been made perfect, those who are entirely sanctified, remain at rest with the perfect love of God.

That's the kind of perfection God wants to give us in this life. That's how far God wants to take us. God wants us to so perfectly love God that we come to rest.

Now, if entire sanctification is perfect love of God, obviously this isn't something we are capable of doing on our own. Just like justification and new birth, entire sanctification is the gift of God. The entire Wesleyan way aims at coming to this final point of rest and true happiness. But just like justification and new birth, coming to this final point isn't really about us working toward it. It is about us letting God work on us, to draw us closer to Him.

Becoming like God, becoming holy, having perfect love of God, is *the whole work* of God and *wholly the work* of God. It is the whole work of God in us—that which all God's work is finally aimed at. And it is wholly the work of God—it is done by God alone. Because of this, everything we Wesleyans do is not so much about doing good things for God. Everything we do is about making ourselves available for God to work on us. They are about recognizing we are powerless without God's work to justify and sanctify us. In the lessons to come, we'll talk more about some of the key things we do, some key practices, as we travel the Wesleyan way to holiness.

QUESTIONS FOR DISCUSSION

1. What is entire sanctification?

2. How are happiness and holiness related? Can we really be happy if we don't get to enjoy the pleasures of sin once in a while?

3. John Wesley had high expectations for sanctification. How can having similarly high expectations change the way we live?

UNIT 3:

WHAT DO WESLEYANS DO?

LESSON 10

What Are Sacraments?

What do people on the Wesleyan way to holiness actually do? What are our key practices?

Some of the things we do are the usual church things. We go to worship together. We pray, both alone and together in church. We read Scripture, again alone and together. We serve others. We give things to those in need. We walk the Wesleyan way when we're alone. And we walk the Wesleyan way when we're together.

One thing we do when we are together are what we call the sacraments. We are baptized and we take Communion. Though you may not realize it, when we do those things, we are traveling down the Wesleyan way. In fact, these two activities both teach and guide us down the Wesleyan way even before we realize it.

It's kind of like getting your driver's license. Long before you learn to drive, you have been growing into the idea of driving. You ride along, becoming accustomed to the bumps, the drifts, the way the body leans into turns. You have seen signs glide by and waited for lights to change. You've heard the exclamations of a missed turn.

You know the feeling of brakes gripping when someone cuts into your lane unannounced. Long before you learn to drive, you've been doing lots of activities associated with driving.

When you get behind the wheel, many things change, but many things stay the same. Though you don't think about it, you lean into turns, which happens to be even more helpful when steering. When you start driving, you discover that when you were just going along for the ride, you learned all sorts of things you can now put to use in a deeper way.

When you get your driver's license, you have to take a written exam. You get a book to study, and you learn a lot about driving you may or may not have noticed before. But once you read the book, you suddenly start seeing things you never knew to look for before. You notice signs, different kinds of intersections, distances between vehicles.

Learning about the Wesleyan way, as we have done in the past five chapters, is kind of like reading the textbook you study for your driver's license test. Once you've learned the Wesleyan way, you can make all kinds of new connections. And each time you take Communion or see a baptism, you can learn even more.

Baptism teaches us about justification and new birth, and Communion teaches us about sanctification. ⚙

At every baptism, three things happen. First, you say two important things: "I repent of my sin, and I believe in the Christian faith." Second, water is applied by dunking, pouring, or sprinkling. Third, the pastor lays hands on you and prays that "the Holy Spirit work within you."

You need all three for a baptism. A baptism without repentance and confession of faith wouldn't really be a baptism. It would just be a bath. A baptism without water would just be a chat and a prayer. And a baptism without the prayer for the Holy

Spirit is incomplete. Why? Because we need justification *and new birth*. We need to be born again, born of the Spirit.

Like we said earlier, we don't just need to have our sins washed away. If that's all that baptism is about, then we would be just like the vampire who feels bad for killing the girl's father, but can't change anything about his appetites. The vampire needs *new* appetites. Likewise, we need a new life, one with the power to overcome sin. We need to be born again, born of the Spirit. Wesleyan baptism teaches us this.

Imagine your pastor is going to baptize you by immersion. Immersion just means the water will be applied by immersing, or dunking, the whole person underwater and then pulling them back up. But what would happen if they did everything in good order, but stopped too early? Imagine: the words of repentance and confession of faith are recited. The pastor dunks you underwater. But then, everything stops, and no one pulls you back up. You go under, but you don't come back up. This is a big problem. You're going to drown! Your old life has ended, but your new life has not begun!

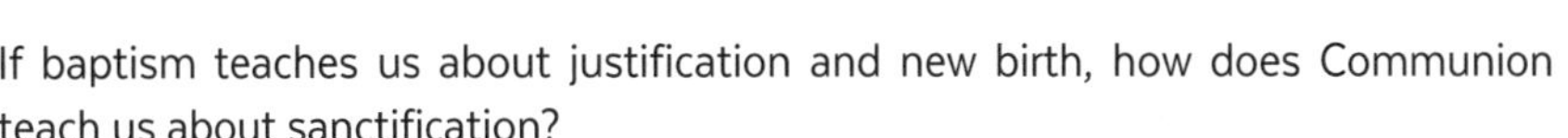

Going under and not coming back up is a bit like being justified without a new birth. You need to go down, and then get pulled back up and set out on new life in the Spirit. You need to be born again; otherwise, you are just dead to sin, but not alive in Christ.

If baptism teaches us about justification and new birth, how does Communion teach us about sanctification?

Remember earlier we said that sanctification is about becoming holy. That is, sanctification is becoming like God, who alone is holy. The key to this is the gift of the Holy Spirit.

Among many other things, Communion teaches us about this gift of the Holy Spirit. One of the most important moments in the Communion is when the pastor prays for the Spirit to be poured out.

Just before the prayer for the Spirit, the pastor reminds us of Jesus' words to His disciples at the first Communion: "Take, eat; this is my body. . . . Drink from it, all of you" (Matt. 26:26–27). Then, we together proclaim our faith: "Christ has died; Christ is risen; Christ will come again." Immediately after that, in one of the most historic moments in Christian practice, the pastor prays over the bread and wine a very special prayer:

> Pour out your Holy Spirit on us gathered here,
> and on these gifts of bread and wine.
> Make them be for us the body and blood of Christ,
> that we might be for the world the body of Christ,
> redeemed by his blood.

"Pour out your Holy Spirit." There is no better way to ask for sanctification. In that moment, those of us on the Wesleyan way give our clearest demonstration of how we become holy. Becoming holy is becoming like Christ (that we might be for the world the body of Christ) by the power of the Holy Spirit.

There are many more things we can learn about sanctification and the Wesleyan way by paying attention to Communion. We Wesleyans will continue celebrating Communion until Christ returns, because we can always learn and experience something new in it. Christ waits there, always ready to give us the Holy Spirit.

Baptism and Communion teach us about the Wesleyan way. But Wesleyans don't believe baptism and Communion just teach us about the Wesleyan way. Certainly they teach us, but they do more than that. Wesleyans believe baptism teaches us about justification and new birth, and it can bring about justification and new birth. And Wesleyans believe Communion teaches us about sanctification, and can bring about sanctification.

How can they *bring about* justification, new birth, and sanctification? John Wesley summed up this basic idea with the phrase "means of grace." A means of grace is something that brings us grace, a thing that God regularly uses to give us grace. But what is grace?

It's sort of like this. Imagine one Christmas you get the coolest LEGO airplane of all time. You unwrap the gift, and after hopping up and down with excitement, you run to your room and start building. You take your time, checking page after page to make sure it's just right. Once it's done, you parade it around with pride. It's easily your favorite toy.

But then you forget to put it up while you go outside to play in the snow. And while you're out, your little sister finds it, and tears it to pieces. Not just that, she also finds the instruction booklet, and tosses it in the fireplace.

Now you're in trouble. It doesn't matter how much your parents punish her. You don't have the instructions, and you can't build your plane again. It's too complicated to remember. You try, but the wings don't look quite right. The weight ends up distributed funny, so it falls over and falls apart.

This is sort of the problem we find ourselves in after sin. We've been busted up and we don't know how to put things back together. Grace is a gift, but a particular kind of gift. Grace is the gift that puts us back together, but doesn't stop at that. It puts us back together and then takes us someplace we had no idea we could go before-hand. It's kind of like Jesus showing up at your house, putting your LEGO plane back together, and then surprising you when He makes it fly! Grace is putting us back together the way we were originally, but then putting that original good condition to a use we had no idea possible. It's putting us together so that we can become holy, just as God is holy!

The means of grace teach us this lesson. Baptism and Communion teach us that this is what God is doing, through grace, in our life. But they don't just teach. They are also the means, or ways, through which God really puts us back together and then makes us holy like Jesus.

The means of grace aren't only like a sign on the interstate, telling you about a place you could go. They're more like the interstate itself, taking you there. They are the ways we become holy like Jesus, and because they are the way to Jesus, they also teach us about that way.

One of the great insights of John Wesley was that God wants to use many means, or ways, to share grace with us. He gives us Scripture, prayer, worship, the sacraments, and opportunities to sacrifice for others. All of them lead us along the way to holiness. All of them lead us to Jesus, and make us more like Him.

QUESTIONS FOR DISCUSSION

1. What is the meaning of baptism? Why is it important? Have you been baptized?

2. What is the meaning of Communion? Why is it important? How often do you take Communion?

3. How do the two sacraments of the church help us to live the Christian life? How are the "forms" of Christian life and the power of the Spirit connected?

What Are Classes and Bands?

"Come, let us join our friends above
who have obtained the prize,
and on the eagle wings of love
to joys celestial rise.
Let saints on earth unite to sing
with those to glory gone,
for all the servants of our King
in earth and heaven are one."

—Charles Wesley, "Come, Let Us Join Our Friends Above"

When Jesus came, He didn't just teach one person. He taught a group of disciples. When the Spirit fell at Pentecost, it didn't just fall on one person. The Spirit fell on a group of disciples. The Bible teaches us that God has always wanted a people, a family. God wants to make us friends, with Himself and with one another.

The way of holiness is a way of *friendship*.

We can see this in baptism and Communion. When we are baptized, we are born by the Spirit into a new family, the church. Christians call one another brother and sister. Communion is a family feast. We share one table, just like a big family at the holidays.

The Wesleyan way of holiness isn't meant to be traveled alone, because our relationship to one another is connected with our relationship to God.

Picture a bicycle wheel, with an outer rim, a hub at the center, and lots of spokes connecting the rim to the center. Imagine God is the hub at the center, and we all stand on the spokes, midway from the hub and the wheel. We are separated from God, yet oriented to God. We are separated by sin from the relationship with God we are intended for, the relationship that will make us happy and at peace and rest. The most important question is: Which way will we go?

Will we draw closer to God, moving along the spoke of the wheel toward the hub, or will we drift further away toward the tire?

Early Christian monks made an important observation about this decision. Whether or not we move toward God, toward the hub, will shape our relationship with each other. This is because the only path to the friendship with one another that we really desire comes by drawing close to God. The spokes meet at the hub, not the

wheel. It's only by coming into connection with God, becoming holy, that it becomes possible to be truly satisfyingly connected to one another.

Sometimes we think we are getting closer to our friends by moving away from God. But this is impossible. The further you move toward the tire, the further you move away from God. And the further you move away from God, the further you get from the one point where you can actually be connected.

The way of holiness is a way of friendship. Holiness makes us better friends. And true friendship helps to make us holy.

One thing that made John Wesley so effective was how well he understood this idea. It shaped how he lived the Christian life, and how he taught others to live the Christian life. The Wesleyan way is a way of friendship.

When Methodism started out, it wasn't a new church. It was a group of church-going Christians seeking to grow closer to God through fellowship. John Wesley and his group of friends at the University of Oxford started out by building friendships centered on common love, worship, and service to God. Others called them Bible Moths and Methodists. But they liked the term Holy Club—they were a group of friends united in their pursuit of the Holy God.

The center of the Methodist movement wasn't John Wesley's field preaching that drew tens of thousands. George Whitefield preached to much larger crowds than Wesley, but left no movement like Wesley's. Late in his life, it is said that Whitefield mourned that his people fell apart like a "rope of sand." But Wesley's held together. Why? Because the center of the Methodist movement was the careful way Wesley developed Christian friendship among Methodists. He called those carefully developed friendships "Societies."

Homes have different rooms and spaces. The further you enter a house, the more you get to know those who live there. We can understand the Wesleyan Societies by thinking about three parts of a home.

First, the porch. We sit on the porch to get to know one another better. We discuss our interests, find common ones, and learn more about one another. The Society meeting in early Methodism was kind of like that. There, Methodists met each week to read Scripture together, sing spiritual songs, and encourage each other in the faith.

Second, the living room. When we invite someone into our living room, we welcome them into our home. We let them look at our stuff. They can see what's important to us. They might see a bunch of books on shelves. They might see a television and a gaming console. They will probably see family photos, or paintings, or special

mementos. They will get to know more about what we're about. Class meetings were sort of like this. Early Methodists, gathered in Classes, would ask one another: "How is it with your soul? Where have you met Christ this week?" They would show one another what God was doing in their lives. ✹

Third, the bedroom. While we might invite someone into our living room, we usually don't invite them into our bedroom. The bedroom is often a messy, intimate place. It's where we throw the piles of laundry when guests are over. It's where to go to hide, to be alone. It's where we are most ourselves, with our problems and frustrations and temptations. The Band meetings were where early Methodists asked one another five hard questions:

1. What known sins have you committed since our last meeting?
2. What temptations have you met with?
3. How were you delivered?
4. What have you thought, said, or done, of which you doubt whether it be sin or not?
5. Have you nothing you desire to keep secret? ✹

Those are intense questions. Methodists gathered in small groups of five to seven, men with men and women with women, and answered these questions as honestly as possible every week. It's kind of like welcoming someone into the bedroom of your soul without cleaning it up. But that's the whole point: to make true friends, friends with those who know the true you.

Friendship with God and friendship with others go together. Just as Methodists believe God wants to make us really holy, like God is holy, so we believe that God wants to make us true friends with one another. And so, a big part of the power of the Wesleyan way is its demand that we share ourselves with one another.

Think about it like this: when Jesus came, He didn't sit alone all the time, popping up occasionally to tell us things. He always gathered a group of people around Him.

He had His closest friends, the twelve disciples, who lived with Him, ate with Him, prayed with Him. He saw everything they did, and they saw everything He did. They were there when He prayed in the garden. And they were there when He resurrected and appeared in the room with them. Jesus' life on earth was a life filled with friendship. When God comes and shows us how we should live, when Jesus shows us the most perfect human life, it is a life marked by friendship with each other.

Now, these Societies, Classes, and Bands will probably sound unfamiliar to you. You are probably familiar with lots of different groups in your churches—Bible studies, Sunday school, youth groups, softball teams, and so on. But I bet you've never been to a Society, Class, or Band meeting before. Over time, Methodists slowly began to do other practices. But anywhere the Wesleyan way has been practiced at its best, it has been built on these kinds of exercises of friendship, all the way down to the raw, bedroom-intimate, Band meeting confessions.

So maybe you need to go looking to build these kinds of friendships. Thankfully, Wesley left behind a good, clear model for us. If you're already a part of the church, then you do a lot of the Society meeting stuff. You share concerns, hear the Word taught, read Scripture together, and sing praise to our God. But now you want to go further. So how can you bring the spirit of the Class meeting into your life? You need to start having conversations about God with your Christian friends. Not conversations about God with non-Christians, which is also good, but the Society is about seeking God in our lives together.

And once you start doing that with all your Christian friends, you can start looking for an opportunity to connect with a smaller group, a group that you can band together with, and there start asking one another the really hard questions. Take a look at those five questions earlier and try asking them to each other. Learn to look for sin, and offer it to God together. Like the early monks, you will find that you grow closer to God and closer to one another. And as you become more holy, you will become better friends.

QUESTIONS FOR DISCUSSION

1. How does getting closer to God help us to get closer to each other? How does getting closer to each other help us to get closer to God?

2. How does your church community shape your life? What groups are you a part of that help you to become more like Jesus?

3. Do you have any friends that are able to challenge you? Are there any parts of your life that you are afraid to let others know about? What can you do about this?

What Happened after Wesley?

> "His kingdom cannot fail,
> He rules o'er earth and heav'n;
> The keys of death and hell
> Are to our Jesus giv'n"
>
> —Charles Wesley, "Rejoice, the Lord Is King"

We have learned about John Wesley's life, about his ministry, and about the growth of Methodism. We have learned the Wesleyan way of salvation, and key Wesleyan practices like the sacraments, and Class and Band meetings. But the story doesn't end with Wesley—it makes its way to us, and becomes our own story.

Late in Wesley's life, he faced a very difficult decision. All his life he had remained a faithful priest in the Church of England. He was an Englishman, and he loved his country. So long as America remained a part of England, Wesley thought the Methodists in America should remain members of the Church of England.

But on July 4, 1776, everything changed. When the Second Continental Congress gathered in Philadelphia, Pennsylvania, and signed the Declaration of Independence, thereby declaring the thirteen English colonies to be independent states, Wesley's arguments for keeping Methodism inside the Church of England broke down. Something had to change.

In America, the situation was dire for the Methodists. During the American Revolution, the Church of England became much smaller relatively quickly. The decline of the Church of England came at the same time Methodism was growing in America. As Methodists grew, it became harder and harder for them to find priests of the Church of England to perform baptisms, serve Communion, and bury their dead. Methodists in America had a crisis.

In December 1784, the crisis was solved with the creation of the Methodist Episcopal Church. The Methodist Episcopal Church adopted Wesley's teaching and way of life. Once established, they went about organizing the unique environment that was North America in the late eighteenth century. As a result, Methodism in North America boomed.

And what was the unique environment of late eighteenth-century North America?

First of all, it was mostly a wilderness frontier. While many of the colonies along the Atlantic Ocean were well established, things changed dramatically inland. In order to spread the good news of Jesus Christ and teach the Wesleyan way of following Him, Methodists took to horseback and traveled huge circuits, or loops, preaching, teaching, baptizing, and celebrating Communion. Early Methodist preachers were notable for their bravery on horseback, spreading the Wesleyan way far into what we think of as the southern states, and west into the wilderness of North America.

As it turned out, those brave preachers were just the thing Methodism needed. While Methodism grew at a steady, moderate rate in the North, it boomed in the South and West.

When the Methodist Episcopal Church was formed in 1784, the membership totaled to no more than 18,000. Six years later, in 1790, there were 58,000 members. By 1804, it numbered 115,000 members.

The first half of the 1800s was a period of great increase in American Methodism. Along the way, the church saw several divisions, most significantly between Southern and Northern Methodists in 1844. But growth continued, and by the time they reunited in 1939, there were more than seven million Methodists in America. How did things get so big?

It was not only the boldness of the preachers that spread Methodism across America—it was the power of their message. Just as in the fields of England where Wesley preached, revival was breaking out in the American frontiers where the Methodists were preaching. This was especially true in the South.

Recall the story of John Wesley and George Whitefield preaching in the fields. They looked around and saw where people were, and told them about the good news of Jesus Christ. God blessed it, and a movement so big that we call it the First Great Awakening broke out. Many people turned to God. Many lives were changed. Many families were saved. People were freed from their addictions. Even the English slave trade came to an end thanks to the efforts of early Methodists!

The story of the Wesleyan way in America is like the revival in England in some ways. The early 1800s was a period of great revival for American Christians, Methodists, and many others. In fact, so many Americans turned to Christ that we now call the early 1800s the Second Great Awakening. Once again, lives were changed, families were saved, people were freed from their addictions, and the Methodists boomed.

In the First Great Awakening, what set the Methodists apart was John Wesley's careful way of organizing those who were stirred up by field preaching into communities (Societies, Classes, and Bands) so they could grow along the Wesleyan way. Likewise, while early American Methodists were leading revivals, they were also developing their own unique practices to live out the Wesleyan way in America.

Francis Asbury is a good example of the way early American Methodists lived out the Wesleyan way. When Asbury arrived in America, it was hard to grow churches. Most Americans lived in small, rural areas, in towns of only a couple thousand people, or out on homesteads. In light of this challenge, Asbury organized all these small towns into circuits, big loops that a Methodist preacher could travel on horseback. The preacher would travel round and round the circuit, organizing the people at each stop, preaching and teaching, baptizing new Christians and babies, and serving Communion. He may not make it back for a few weeks, and so one of the most important tasks for the traveling preacher would be to oversee the Class leaders, people in the local communities who would lead Class meetings during the weeks between the preacher's visits. Asbury not only organized the circuits, but he was relentless in riding them. In fact, it is estimated that he rode on horseback and in carriages 300,000 miles over his lifetime—that's about twelve loops around the earth!

This system was extremely effective. Methodism boomed in the first half of the nineteenth century, growing so quickly that, if it had continued at the same pace from 1850–1900, there would have been more Methodists than Americans!

Just like Wesley preached in the fields and organized the early Methodists into Societies, Classes, and Bands to live out the Wesleyan way, American Methodists in the Second Great Awakening reached people through revivals and camp meetings and then placed them in communities. The Wesleyan way was revived in a new form, but it followed the same principles.

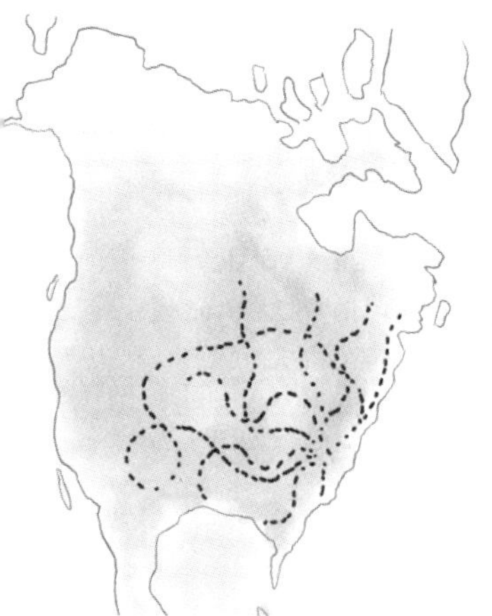

We need you to revive the Wesleyan way. We invite you to take it up, to study it, and, most important, to live it out. You will need to continue the teachings and practices that we are giving you, but you will also need to figure out how to live the Wesleyan way in your own time and place.

Imagine a teacher assigns you a book report. Your teacher might give you several instructions. She might say, "It will be necessary for you to read the book carefully, and to take careful notes, in order to write a good book report." This is true. These things are necessary for a good book report; but if that is all you do, you won't have a book report. You'll just have a pile of notes. Though they are necessary, they are not sufficient. Good book reports won't exist without careful reading, but neither will they exist without good writing.

What we've taught you here are several things necessary for the Wesleyan way. If you don't have these pieces, you won't be pursuing Christ the way Wesley handed down to the early Methodists; but to say they are necessary isn't to say they are sufficient. You need more than just what we've handed you here.

Here's what we know. The Wesleyan way has a few fundamental features. There is power in the way of salvation you have learned, and in the means of grace we've discussed. Whatever you do going forward, you need to do those practices—go to church, read Scripture, pray, remember your baptism, celebrate Communion, form spiritual relationships, confess your sins, and hold each other accountable.

But you will need a lot more than just this to live out the Wesleyan way. We do not know what questions may arise for you, or what opportunities may present themselves. We need you to live out the Wesleyan way, whatever may come your way. Whatever you face, looking back at these necessary lessons will help you figure out how to carry on the faith into the future.

John Wesley started an important movement, and there will probably always be people who call themselves Wesleyans, or Methodists, much like there will probably always be people who call themselves Platonists, or Buddhists. But Wesley didn't want his name to survive; he wanted the Wesleyan way, the Methodist methods, both the forms and the power, to survive:

> I am not afraid that the people called Methodists should ever cease to exist either in Europe or America. But I am afraid lest they should only exist as a dead sect,

having the form of religion without the power. And this undoubtedly will be the case unless they hold fast both the doctrine, spirit, and discipline with which they first set out. ✦

Welcome to the Wesleyan way. Cling to the forms you've learned. Discover the power. May it bring you new life. May you care for it. May you hand it on to the ones who come after.

QUESTIONS FOR DISCUSSION

1. Why was the Methodist movement so impactful? How did John Wesley's legacy change the church?

2. Where do you see the Christian church failing to carry out God's mission?

3. How are you carrying on the Wesleyan way? What do you think God wants you to do to help spread God's kingdom on earth?

Sermon 43: The Scripture Way of Salvation

Note: We have included John Wesley's Sermon 43: The Scripture Way of Salvation as a supplement to The Absolute Basics of the Wesleyan Way *for two reasons. First, it is the richest explanation of Wesley's teaching on the order of salvation that we have attempted to explain in Unit 2 of this book. Second, we wanted to offer our readers an easy and direct way to sample the work of John Wesley. Here you can not only learn more about Wesley's view of salvation, but you can hear a bit of the tone of his preaching and writing.*

- -

"Ye are saved through faith." —Ephesians 2:8.

1. Nothing can be more intricate, complex, and hard to be understood, than religion, as it has been often described. And this is not only true concerning the religion of the Heathens, even many of the wisest of them, but concerning the religion of those also who were, in some sense, Christians; yea, and men of great name in the Christian world; men who seemed to be pillars thereof. Yet how easy to be understood, how plain and simple a thing, is the genuine religion of Jesus Christ; provided only that we take it in its native form, just as it is described in the oracles of God! It is exactly suited, by the wise Creator and Governor of the world, to the weak understanding and narrow capacity of man in his present state. How observable is this, both with regard to the end it proposes, and the means to attain that end! The end is, in one word, salvation; the means to attain it, faith.

2. It is easily discerned, that these two little words, I mean faith and salvation, include the substance of all the Bible, the marrow, as it were, of the whole Scripture. So much the more should we take all possible care to avoid all mistake concerning them, and to form a true and accurate judgment concerning both the one and the other.

3. Let us then seriously inquire,
    I. What is Salvation?
    II. What is that faith whereby we are saved?
    And, III. How are we saved by it?

I.

1. And, first, let us inquire, What is salvation? The salvation which is here spoken of is not what is frequently understood by that word, the going to heaven, eternal happiness. It is not the soul's going to paradise, termed by our Lord, "Abraham's bosom." It is not a blessing which lies on the other side death; or, as we usually speak, in the other world. The very words of the text itself put this beyond all question: "You are saved." It is not something at a distance: it is a present thing; a blessing which, through the free mercy of God, you are now in possession of. Nay, the words may be rendered, and that with equal propriety, "You have been saved": so that the salvation which is here spoken of might be extended to the entire work of God, from the first dawning of grace in the soul, till it is consummated in glory.

2. If we take this in its utmost extent, it will include all that is wrought in the soul by what is frequently termed "natural conscience," but more properly, "preventing grace";—all the drawings of the Father; the desires after God, which, if we yield to them, increase more and more;—all that light wherewith the Son of God "enlightens every one that comes into the world"; showing every man "to do justly, to love mercy, and to walk humbly with his God";—all the convictions which His Spirit, from time to time, works in every child of man—although it is true, the generality of men stifle them as soon as possible, and after a while forget, or at least deny, that they ever had them at all.

3. But we are at present concerned only with that salvation which the Apostle is directly speaking of. And this consists of two general parts, justification and sanctification. Justification is another word for pardon. It is the forgiveness of all our sins; and, what is necessarily implied therein, our acceptance with God. The price whereby this has been procured for us (commonly termed "the meritorious cause of our justification"), is the blood and righteousness of Christ; or, to express it a little more clearly, all that Christ has done and suffered for us, till He "poured out His soul for the transgressors." The immediate effects of justification are, the peace of God, a "peace that passes all understanding," and a "rejoicing in hope of the glory of God" "with joy unspeakable and full of glory."

4. And at the same time that we are justified, yea, in that very moment, sanctification begins. In that instant we are born again, born from above, born of the Spirit: there is a real as well as a relative change. We are inwardly renewed by the power of God. We feel "the love of God shed abroad in our heart by the Holy Spirit which is given unto us"; producing love to all mankind, and more especially to the children of God; expelling the love of the world, the love of pleasure, of ease, of honor, of money, together with pride, anger, self-will, and every other evil temper; in a word, changing the earthly, sensual, devilish mind, into "the mind which was in Christ Jesus."

5. How naturally do those who experience such a change imagine that all sin is gone; that it is utterly rooted out of their heart, and has no more any place therein! How easily do they draw that inference, "I feel no sin; therefore, I have none: it does not stir; therefore it does not exist: it has no motion; therefore, it has no being!"

6. But it is seldom long before they are undeceived, finding sin was only suspended, not destroyed. Temptations return, and sin revives; showing it was but stunned before, not dead. They now feel two principles in themselves, plainly contrary to each other; "the flesh lusting against the Spirit"; nature opposing the grace of God. They cannot deny, that although they still feel power to believe in Christ, and to love God; and although His "Spirit" still "witnesses with their spirits, that they are children of God"; yet they feel in themselves sometimes pride or

self-will, sometimes anger or unbelief. They find one or more of these frequently stirring in their heart, though not conquering; yea, perhaps, "thrusting sore at them that they may fall"; but the Lord is their help.

7. How exactly did Macarius, fourteen hundred years ago, describe the present experience of the children of God: "The unskilful," or unexperienced, "when grace operates, presently imagine they have no more sin. Whereas they that have discretion cannot deny, that even we who have the grace of God may be molested again. For we have often had instances of some among the brethren, who have experienced such grace as to affirm that they had no sin in them; and yet, after all, when they thought themselves entirely freed from it, the corruption that lurked within was stirred up anew, and they were wellnigh burned up."

8. From the time of our being born again, the gradual work of sanctification takes place. We are enabled "by the Spirit" to "mortify the deeds of the body," of our evil nature; and as we are more and more dead to sin, we are more and more alive to God. We go on from grace to grace, while we are careful to "abstain from all appearance of evil," and are "zealous of good works," as we have opportunity, doing good to all men; while we walk in all His ordinances blameless, therein worshipping Him in spirit and in truth; while we take up our cross, and deny ourselves every pleasure that does not lead us to God.

9. It is thus that we wait for entire sanctification; for a full salvation from all our sins,—from pride, self-will, anger, unbelief; or, as the Apostle expresses it, "go unto perfection." But what is perfection? The word has various senses: here it means perfect love. It is love excluding sin; love filling the heart, taking up the whole capacity of the soul. It is love "rejoicing evermore, praying without ceasing, in everything giving thanks."

II.

But what is faith through which we are saved? This is the second point to be considered.

1. Faith, in general, is defined by the Apostle as, the evidence of things unseen. An evidence, a divine evidence and conviction (the word means both) of things not

seen; not visible, not perceivable either by sight, or by any other of the external senses. It implies both a supernatural evidence of God, and of the things of God; a kind of spiritual light exhibited to the soul, and a supernatural sight or perception thereof. Accordingly, the Scripture speaks of God's giving sometimes light, sometimes a power of discerning it. So St. Paul: "God, who commanded light to shine out of darkness, has shined in our hearts, to give us the light of the knowledge of the glory of God in the face of Jesus Christ." And elsewhere the same Apostle speaks of "the eyes of" our "understanding being opened." By this two-fold operation of the Holy Spirit, having the eyes of our soul both opened and enlightened, we see the things which the natural "eye has not seen, neither the ear heard." We have a prospect of the invisible things of God; we see the spiritual world, which is all round about us, and yet no more discerned by our natural faculties than if it had no being. And we see the eternal world; piercing through the veil which hangs between time and eternity. Clouds and darkness then rest upon it no more, but we already see the glory which shall be revealed.

2. Taking the word in a more particular sense, faith is a divine evidence and conviction not only that "God was in Christ, reconciling the world unto Himself," but also that Christ loved me, and gave Himself for me. It is by this faith (whether we term it the essence, or rather a property thereof) that we receive Christ; that we receive Him in all His offices, as our Prophet, Priest, and King. It is by this that He is "made of God unto us wisdom, and righteousness, and sanctification, and redemption."

3. "But is this the faith of assurance, or faith of adherence?" The Scripture mentions no such distinction. The Apostle says, "There is one faith, and one hope of our calling"; one Christian, saving faith; "as there is one Lord," in whom we believe, and "one God and Father of us all." And it is certain, this faith necessarily implies an assurance (which is here only another word for evidence, it being hard to tell the difference between them) that Christ loved me, and gave Himself for me. For "he that believes" with the true living faith "has the witness in himself"; "the Spirit witnesses with his spirit that he is a child of God." "Because he is a son, God has sent forth the Spirit of His Son into his heart, crying, Abba, Father"; giving him an assurance that he is so, and a childlike confidence in Him. But let it be observed, that, in the very nature of the thing, the assurance goes before the confidence. For a man cannot have a childlike confidence in God till he knows he

is a child of God. Therefore, confidence, trust, reliance, adherence, or whatever else it be called, is not the first, as some have supposed, but the second, branch or act of faith.

4. It is by this faith we are saved, justified, and sanctified; taking that word in its highest sense. But how are we justified and sanctified by faith? This is our third head of inquiry. And this being the main point in question, and a point of no ordinary importance, it will not be improper to have it a more distinct and particular consideration.

III.

1. And, first, how are we justified by faith? In what sense is this to be understood? I answer, faith is the condition, and the only condition, of justification. It is the condition: none is justified but he that believes: without faith no man is justified. And it is the only condition: this alone is sufficient for justification. Every one that believes is justified, whatever else he has or has not. In other words: no man is justified till he believes; every man when he believes is justified.

2. "But does not God command us to repent also yea, and to 'bring forth fruits meet for repentance'—to cease, for instance, from doing evil, and learn to do well? And is not both the one and the other of the utmost necessity, insomuch that if we willingly neglect either, we cannot reasonably expect to be justified at all? But if this be so, how can it be said that faith is the only condition of justification?" God does undoubtedly command us both to repent, and to bring forth fruits meet for repentance; which if we willingly neglect, we cannot reasonably expect to be justified at all: therefore both repentance, and fruits meet for repentance, are, in some sense, necessary to justification. But they are not necessary in the same sense with faith, nor in the same degree. Not in the same degree; for those fruits are only necessary conditionally; if there be time and opportunity for them. Otherwise a man may be justified without them, as was the thief upon the cross (if we may call him so; for a late writer has discovered that he was no thief, but a very honest and respectable person!); but he cannot be justified without faith; this is impossible. Likewise, let a man have ever so much repentance, or ever so many of the fruits meet for repentance, yet all this does not at all avail;

he is not justified till he believes. But the moment he believes, with or without those fruits, yea, with more or less repentance, he is justified. —Not in the same sense; for repentance and its fruits are only remotely necessary; necessary in order to faith; whereas faith is immediately necessary to justification. It remains, that faith is the only condition, which is immediately and proximately necessary to justification.

3. "But do you believe we are sanctified by faith? We know you believe that we are justified by faith; but do not you believe, and accordingly teach, that we are sanctified by our works?" So it has been roundly and vehemently affirmed for these five-and-twenty years: but I have constantly declared just the contrary; and that in all manner of ways. I have continually testified in private and in public, that we are sanctified as well as justified by faith. And indeed the one of those great truths does exceedingly illustrate the other. Exactly as we are justified by faith, so are we sanctified by faith. Faith is the condition, and the only condition, of sanctification, exactly as it is of justification. It is the condition: none is sanctified but he that believes; without faith no man is sanctified. And it is the only condition: this alone is sufficient for sanctification. Every one that believes is sanctified, whatever else he has or has not. In other words, no man is sanctified till he believes; every man when he believes is sanctified.

4. "But is there not a repentance consequent upon, as well as a repentance previous to, justification? And is it not incumbent on all that are justified to be 'zealous of good works'? Yea, are not these so necessary, that if a man willingly neglect them he cannot reasonably expect that he shall ever be sanctified in the full sense; that is, perfected in love? Nay, can he grow at all in grace, in the loving knowledge of our Lord Jesus Christ? Yea, can he retain the grace which God has already given him? Can he continue in the faith which he has received, or in the favor of God? Do not you yourself allow all this, and continually assert it? But, if this be so, how can it be said that faith is the only condition of sanctification?"

5. I do allow all this, and continually maintain it as the truth of God. I allow there is a repentance consequent upon, as well as a repentance previous to, justification. It is incumbent on all that are justified to be zealous of good works. And they are so necessary, that if a man willingly neglect them, he cannot reasonably

expect that he shall ever be sanctified; he cannot grow in grace, in the image of God, the mind which was in Christ Jesus; nay, he cannot retain the grace he has received; he cannot continue in faith, or in the favor of God. What is the inference we must draw here from? Why, that both repentance, rightly understood, and the practice of all good works,—works of piety, as well as works of mercy (now properly so called, since they spring from faith), are, in some sense, necessary to sanctification.

6. I say, "repentance rightly understood"; for this must not be confounded with the former repentance. The repentance consequent upon justification is widely different from that which is antecedent to it. This implies no guilt, no sense of condemnation, no consciousness of the wrath of God. It does not suppose any doubt of the favor of God, or any "fear that has torment." It is properly a conviction, wrought by the Holy Spirit, of the sin which still remains in our heart; of the carnal mind, which "does still remain" (as our Church speaks) "even in them that are regenerate"; although it does no longer reign; it has not now dominion over them. It is a conviction of our proneness to evil, of an heart bent to backsliding, of the still continuing tendency of the flesh to lust against the spirit. Sometimes, unless we continually watch and pray, it lusts to pride, sometimes to anger, sometimes to love of the world, love of ease, love of honor, or love of pleasure more than of God. It is a conviction of the tendency of our heart to self-will, to Atheism, or idolatry; and above all, to unbelief; whereby, in a thousand ways, and under a thousand pretenses, we are ever departing, more or less, from the living God.

7. With this conviction of the sin remaining in our hearts, there is joined a clear conviction of the sin remaining in our lives; still cleaving to all our words and actions. In the best of these we now discern a mixture of evil, either in the spirit, the matter, or the manner of them; something that could not endure the righteous judgment of God, were He extreme to mark what is done amiss. Where we least suspected it, we find a taint of pride or self-will, of unbelief or idolatry; so that we are now more ashamed of our best duties than formerly of our worst sins; and hence we cannot but feel that these are so far from having anything meritorious in them, yea, so far from being able to stand in sight of the divine justice, that for those also we should be guilty before God, were it not for the blood of the covenant.

8. Experience shows that, together with this conviction of sin remaining in our hearts, and cleaving to all our words and actions; as well as the guilt which on account thereof we should incur, were we not continually sprinkled with the atoning blood; one thing more is implied in this repentance; namely, a conviction of our helplessness, of our utter inability to think one good thought, or to form one good desire; and much more to speak one word aright, or to perform one good action, but through His free, almighty grace, first preventing us, and then accompanying us every moment.

9. "But what good works are those, the practice of which you affirm to be necessary to sanctification?" First, all works of piety; such as public prayer, family prayer, and praying in our closet; receiving the supper of the Lord; searching the Scriptures, by hearing, reading, meditating; and using such a measure of fasting or abstinence as our bodily health allows.

10. Secondly, all works of mercy; whether they relate to the bodies or souls of men; such as feeding the hungry, clothing the naked, entertaining the stranger, visiting those that are in prison, or sick, or variously afflicted; such as the endeavoring to instruct the ignorant, to awaken the stupid sinner, to quicken the lukewarm, to confirm the wavering, to comfort the feeble-minded, to succour the tempted, or contribute in any manner to the saving of souls from death. This is the repentance, and these the "fruits meet for repentance," which are necessary to full sanctification. This is the way wherein God has appointed His children to wait for complete salvation.

11. Hence may appear the extreme mischievousness of that seemingly innocent opinion, that there is no sin in a believer; that all sin is destroyed, root and branch, the moment a man is justified. By totally preventing that repentance, it quite blocks up the way to sanctification. There is no place for repentance in him who believes there is no sin either in his life or heart; consequently, there is no place for his being perfected in love, to which that repentance is indispensably necessary.

12. Hence it may likewise appear, that there is no possible danger in thus expecting full salvation. For suppose we were mistaken, suppose no such blessing ever was or can be attained, yet we lose nothing: nay, that very expectation quickens us in

using all the talents which God has given us; yea, in improving them all; so that when our Lord comes, He will receive His own with increase.

13. But to return, though it be allowed, that both this repentance and its fruits are necessary to full salvation; yet they are not necessary either in the same sense with faith, or in the same degree: —Not in the same degree; for these fruits are only necessary conditionally, if there be time and opportunity for them; otherwise a man may be sanctified without them. But he cannot be sanctified without faith. Likewise, let a man have ever so much of this repentance, or ever so many good works, yet all this does not at all avail; he is not sanctified till he believes. But the moment he believes, with or without those fruits, yea, with more or less of this repentance, he is sanctified. —Not in the same sense; for this repentance and these fruits are only remotely necessary,—necessary in order to the continuance of his faith, as well as the increase of it; whereas faith is immediately and directly necessary to sanctification. It remains, that faith is the only condition which is immediately and proximately necessary to sanctification.

14. "But what is that faith whereby we are sanctified,—saved from sin, and perfected in love?" It is a divine evidence and conviction, first, that God has promised it in the holy Scripture. Till we are thoroughly satisfied of this, there is no moving one step further. And one would imagine there needed not one word more to satisfy a reasonable man of this, than the ancient promise, "Then will I circumcise your heart, and the heart of your seed, to love the Lord your God with all your heart, and with all your soul, and with all your mind." How clearly does this express being perfected in love!—how strongly imply the being saved from all sin! For as long as love takes up the whole heart, what room is there for sin therein?

15. It is a divine evidence and conviction, secondly, that what God has promised He is able to perform. Admitting, therefore, that "with men it is impossible" to "bring a clean thing out of an unclean," to purify the heart from all sin, and to instill it with all holiness; yet this creates no difficulty in the case, seeing "with God all things are possible." And surely no one ever imagined it was possible to any power less than that of the Almighty! But if God speaks, it shall be done. God says, "Let there be light; and there is light"!

16. It is, thirdly, a divine evidence and conviction that He is able and willing to do it now. And why not? Is not a moment to Him the same as a thousand years? He cannot want more time to accomplish whatever is His will. And He cannot want or stay for any more worthiness or fitness in the persons He is pleased to honor. We may therefore boldly say, at any point of time, "Now is the day of salvation!" "To-day, if you will hear His voice, harden not your hearts!" "Behold, all things are now ready; come unto the marriage!"

17. To this confidence, that God is both able and willing to sanctify us now, there needs to be added one thing more,—a divine evidence and conviction that He doeth it. In that hour it is done: God says to the inmost soul, "According to your faith be it unto you!" Then the soul is pure from every spot of sin; it is clean "from all unrighteousness." The believer then experiences the deep meaning of those solemn words, "If we walk in the light as He is in the light, we have fellowship one with another, and the blood of Jesus Christ His Son cleanses us from all sin."

18. "But does God work this great work in the soul gradually or instantaneously?" Perhaps it may be gradually wrought in some; I mean in this sense,—they do not advert to the particular moment wherein sin ceases to be. But it is infinitely desirable, were it the will of God, that it should be done instantaneously; that the Lord should destroy sin "by the breath of His mouth," in a moment, in the twinkling of an eye. And so He generally does; a plain fact, of which there is evidence enough to satisfy any unprejudiced person. You therefore look for it every moment! Look for it in the way above described; in all those good works whereunto you are "created anew in Christ Jesus." Therein then no danger; you can be no worse, if you are no better, for that expectation. For were you to be disappointed of your hope, still you lose nothing. But you shall not be disappointed of your hope: it will come, and will not tarry. Look for it then every day, every hour, every moment! Why not this hour, this moment? Certainly you may look for it now, if you believe it is by faith. And by this token you may surely know whether you seek it by faith or by works. If by works, you want something to be done first, before you are sanctified. You think, I must first be or do thus or thus. Then you are seeking it by works unto this day. If you seek it by faith, you may expect it as you are; and expect it now. It is of importance to observe,

that there is an inseparable connection between these three points,—expect it by faith; expect it as you are; and expect it now! To deny one of them, is to deny them all; to allow one, is to allow them all. Do you believe we are sanctified by faith? Be true then to your principle; and look for this blessing just as you are, neither better nor worse; as a poor sinner that has still nothing to pay, nothing to plead, but "Christ died." And if you look for it as you are, then expect it now. Stay for nothing. Why should you? Christ is ready; and He is all you want. He is waiting for you: He is at the door! Let your inmost soul cry out,

> "Come in, come in, you heavenly Guest!
> Nor hence again remove;
> But sup with me, and let the feast
> Be everlasting love."

Text from John Wesley, "Scripture Way of Salvation," in Thomas Jackson, ed., *The Works of John Wesley*, vol. 7 (London: Conference Office, 1811), 306–18.

NOTES

1 The phrase, "a brand plucked from the fire," in the book of Zechariah is a reference to Joshua, Moses' servant. According to the book of Exodus, after Moses led the people of Israel out of slavery in Egypt, through the Red Sea, they got stuck wandering in the wilderness for forty years. Why? Because they grumbled and didn't believe the promises of God—all of them except Joshua and Moses. But even Moses had to pass before they could enter the promised land. After Moses died, it was Joshua who led the people out of the wilderness and into the promised land. The book of Exodus tells the story of Moses. The book of Joshua tells the story of Joshua. God used Moses to free Israel from slavery. God used Joshua to bring them to their destination in the promised land. *Joshua was one of the people saved from slavery when Moses led them out of Egypt. He was plucked from the fire.* He stayed faithful, while Israel doubted, so he led them to the promised land. Jesus, of course, both saved us from bondage and led us to the promised land; He is the new Moses and the new Joshua. Moses and Joshua were images, figures, partial pictures of Jesus Christ.

2 Richard P. Heitzenrater, *Wesley and the People Called Methodists*, 2nd ed. (Nashville: Abingdon Press, 2013), 51.

3 W. Reginald Ward and Richard P. Heitzenrater, eds., *The Works of John Wesley*, Bicentennial ed., vol. 18, *Journals and Diaries I* (Nashville: Abingdon Press, 1988), 143.

4 For a long time, Methodists have talked about John Wesley's trip to Georgia as if it were an utter failure, and clear evidence of the overall weakness of his faith early in his life. Recently, a very important book was written by Geordan Hammond that suggests we think a little differently about what happened in Georgia. Hammond shows that Wesley's early work in Georgia actually remained important to all of the work that followed. He shows that it wasn't as miserable a failure as some people have suggested. In this book, we try to think about the relationship between what happened early in his life and what came later not in terms of a total transformation, but in terms of old forms gaining power (see the next couple of chapters for what we mean) and new ones being developed. That's our way of saying that Wesley had a lot right about Christianity early in his life, even if what happened later in his life at Aldersgate was significant. If you want a deep dive into these topics, grab a copy of this book: Geordan Hammond, *John Wesley in America: Restoring Primitive Christianity* (Oxford: Oxford University Press, 2016).

5 We're going to be citing from John Wesley's sermons and journals and other writings from time to time. There are two major sources for the writings of John Wesley. The newest and best is the Wesley Works project, or what we call the "Bicentennial Edition" in our notes. It is not yet complete, but nearing completion, and when it is done it will provide high-quality editions of all of John Wesley's works. You can read more about these volumes at: https://wesley-works.org. Since not all of these volumes are currently completed, sometimes we have to rely on older copies of John Wesley's writings, and there we use what we call the "Jackson Edition," edited late in the nineteenth century by Thomas Jackson. If you want to dive into piles of research on the Wesleys, a great place to start is through the website maintained by Duke Divinity School's Center for Studies in the Wesleyan Tradition: https://divinity.duke.edu/initiatives/cswt. Also, if you want a comprehensive bibliography on John Wesley, Kenneth Collins at Asbury Theological Seminary has maintained an excellent source, available for free at https://place.asburyseminary.edu/firstfruitspapers/99/. If you want the best, most academic biography of Wesley, we recommend Henry Rack's *Reasonable Enthusiast: John Wesley and the Rise of Methodism*, 3rd ed. (London: Epworth Press, 2002). A recent, very good, and much shorter book on John Wesley is Henry H. "Hal" Knight's *John Wesley: Optimist of Grace*, Cascade Companions (Eugene, OR: Wipf and Stock, 2018).

LESSON 2: WHAT HAPPENED AT ALDERSGATE?

1 Who were these Moravians? They take their name from the region where they originated, Moravia, in the modern-day Czech Republic. In the fifteenth century, Czech Christians began reforming against the Church of Rome, many years before Martin Luther posted the Ninety-Five Theses and started what we think of as the Protestant Reformation. In 1415, one of the great Czech leaders, Jan Hus, was tried and burned at the stake for preaching against the practices and abuses of the Church of Rome. A few decades later, the Moravian Church emerged to carry on the teaching of Hus and other Czech reformers. The 1500s and 1600s were very difficult for the Moravians, as they were repeatedly exiled and perse-cuted for their faith. They held together, however, and even grew, as they had a passion for spreading their faith from the very beginning. In the 1700s, a great leader, Count Nicholas von Zinzendorf, welcomed Moravians who were fleeing persecution into his estate in Herrnhut, Germany. There the Moravians flourished, enjoyed enough peace to pursue their own practices, and began to send out missionaries all over the world. It was that community at Herrnhut that John Wesley went to visit after his Aldersgate experience.

2 It's not entirely clear, from Charles's Journal, whether or not it was Mrs. Turner or Mrs. Musgrave. You can read the full account in John R. Tyson, ed., *Charles Wesley: A Reader* (Oxford: Oxford University Press, 1989), 98–99.

3 What was it that struck John Wesley in Martin Luther's "Preface to the Epistle to the Romans"? He says it was the description of the change God works in the heart through faith. One striking passage on this point comes relatively early in the Preface. Luther writes:

> Faith is not that human notion and dream that some hold for faith. Because they see that no betterment of life and no good works follow it, and yet they can hear and say much about faith, they fall into error, and say, "Faith is not enough; one must do works in order to be righteous and be saved." This is the reason that, when they hear the Gospel, they fall to—and make for themselves, by their own powers, an idea in their hearts, which says, "I believe." This they hold for true faith. But it is a human imagination and idea that never reaches the depths of the heart, and so nothing comes of it and no betterment follows it. Faith, however, is a divine work in us. It changes us and makes us to be born anew of God (John 1); it kills the old Adam and makes altogether different men, in heart and spirit and mind and powers, and it brings with it the Holy Ghost. O, it is a living, busy, active, mighty thing, this faith; and so it is impossible for it not to do good works incessantly.

Martin Luther, "Preface to the Epistle to the Romans," in *Works of Martin Luther, The Philadelphia Edition*, Vol. 6 (Grand Rapids, MI: Baker Book House, 1982), 451.

4 W. Reginald Ward and Richard P. Heitzenrater, eds., *The Works of John Wesley*, Bicentennial ed., vol. 18, *Journals and Diaries I* (Nashville: Abingdon Press, 1988), 249–50.

5 People have often asked if John Wesley was saved at Aldersgate or if he was saved sometime before. This is a difficult question to answer. Surely something big happened to John Wesley at Aldersgate. He talked about his experience repeatedly later on in his life. But at the same time, he continued a lot of the practices and beliefs he held before his Aldersgate experience. It may help you to think about salvation in two different ways. We can name it as a present experience, of being saved, which is really just a way of talking about the start of a long process that will end when we are finally saved entirely and enter heaven. Or we can name it as that final experience of final salvation, when we enter heaven. While people will debate what happened at Aldersgate, it's important to remember that what John Wesley was always really interested in was not the start of salvation, though he thought it important and had many thoughts on the topic. What kept John Wesley's interest and occupied most of his energy was working toward the goal of final salvation. Aldersgate was an important step on that journey. So was the Holy Club at Oxford. Even the realization of his need for deeper faith while at sea was an important step. All of those were part of the story of his life moving toward final salvation. You probably have lots of stories already that are a part of your own process in moving toward final salvation!

 Ward and Heitzenrater, eds., *Journal*, 18:246.

LESSON 3: WHAT WAS WESLEY LIKE AFTER ALDERSGATE?

The language of "form" and "power" of godliness comes from Paul the apostle's second letter to Timothy (2 Timothy 3:5). In the letter, Paul includes a warning for Timothy and all of those who read his letter. (Paul expected Christians to spread his letters around in the early church so that they could learn more about Jesus. We still spread those letters when we read the Bible!) He warned them about certain kinds of people who will come among them, who will keep "the outward form of godliness," but at the same time "deny its power." He gives a lot of signs to look for, to figure out who these people are, because when it comes to doing the "outward form of godliness" stuff they will look just like you and me. Here are the signs he gives for those who deny the power of godliness:

> For people will be lovers of themselves, lovers of money, boasters, arrogant, abusive, disobedient to their parents, ungrateful, unholy, inhuman, implacable, slanderers, profligates, brutes, haters of good, treacherous, reckless, swollen with conceit, lovers of pleasure rather than lovers of God. (3:2–4)

The problem for Paul, and for Wesley, isn't that these people are doing the forms of godliness. It's that they deny those forms their power by not allowing God to set them free from loving themselves above everything else, rather than loving God above all else. The power of godliness is in its ability to change that thing about us—to make us love God and others above ourselves. That's what the forms are really for.

W. Reginald Ward and Richard P. Heitzenrater, eds., *The Works of John Wesley*, Bicentennial ed., vol. 19, *Journals and Diaries II* (Nashville: Abingdon Press, 1990), 381. Here's the following Wednesday:

Wednesday, March 28.

5.45 (AM) Sang, dressed.

6	Read Prayers; at Betty Hopson's, Mrs. West, Esther, religious talk, tea prayed.
9	At Agutter's, transcribed to Clayton; writ notes.
10.30	Prayed (+)
10.45	Sins!! prayed.
11	Necessary business.
11.30	Walked, meditated.
12	At Islington, necessary talk (religious).
1.15	At Mrs. Sellars', the new band, religious talk, sang.
2	Religious talk with Patterson, prayed.
2.45	At Jewkes', with him at Mrs. May's, necessary talk (religious).
3.15	At Jewkes'.
4	Mason there, tea, religious talk, prayed with Miss Kent.
5.15	At Mrs. West's, tea, religious talk, prayed.
6.30	At home; necessary business.
7	The leaders, prayed, etc.
8	Fetter Lane; talk of my going to Bristol; business.; lots, I going [sic]! prayed.
10.30	At home; supper, necessary talk (religious), prayed.

Wesley consistently rose early (rarely later than 6:00) and was in bed by 11:00, though he did vary his schedule from time to time. Most of his day was taken up with the hard work of overseeing the Methodists and with the religious practices that remained essential to his ministry. He kept a diary and a journal, for distinct purposes. His diary, like the entries above, accounted for his activities each day. His journal was more occasional, and discussed in more detail the major events of his life. On this day, March 28, 1739, he included a long journal entry about his decision to go from London to Bristol, England. In Bristol, he met George Whitefield, who was preaching in the fields to thousands. After a day or so in Bristol, John Wesley decided to preach in the fields like Whitefield, and that was where revivals broke out and the Methodists really boomed. You can read about this time in John's life by flipping between his journal and diary entries in the text previously listed edited by Ward and Heitzenrater.

 Albert C. Outler, ed., *The Works of John Wesley*, Bicentennial ed., vol. 3, *Sermons III* (Nashville: Abingdon Press, 1986), 428.

John Wesley talked a lot about different kinds of faith. Just a few months after Aldersgate, in June 1738, he preached a sermon entitled "Salvation by Faith." There he talked about the faith of a heathen, the faith of a devil (after all, the devil believes in God), the faith of the apostles while Christ lived, and the faith of the Christian. He returned to this theme throughout his ministry. In an important sermon, later in his life (1788), entitled "On Faith," he talked about the relationship between the faith of a servant and the faith of a child (or a son, as he put it). He wrote:

> You have already great reason to praise God that he has called you to his honourable service (that you have the faith of a servant). Fear not. Continue crying unto him; "and you shall see greater things than these." And, indeed, unless the servants of God halt by the way (that is, unless you stop crying out to God for more faith), they will receive the adoption of sons. They will receive the *faith* of the children of God by his *revealing* his only-begotten Son in their hearts. Thus the faith of a child is properly and directly a divine conviction whereby every child of God is enabled to testify, "The life that I now live, I live by faith in the Son of God, who loved me, and gave himself for me." And whosoever hath this, "the Spirit of God witnesseth with his spirit that he is a child of God." So the Apostle writes to the Galatians, "Ye are the sons of God by faith." "And because ye are sons, God hath sent forth the Spirit of his Son into your hearts, crying, 'Abba, Father'"; that is, giving you a childlike confidence in him, together with a kind affection toward him. This then it is that (if St. Paul was taught of God, and wrote as he was moved by the Holy Ghost) properly constitutes the difference between a servant of God and a child of God. "He that believeth", as a child of God "hath the witness in himself." This the servant hath not. Yet let no man discourage him; rather, lovingly exhort him to expect it every moment!

Albert C. Outler, ed., *The Works of John Wesley*, Bicentennial ed., vol. 3, *Sermons III* (Nashville: Abingdon Press, 1986), 497–98.

LESSON 4: WHAT DID JOHN WESLEY DO?

 George Whitefield was one of the greatest preachers of all time. He preached all over the English and North American countryside. Some estimate that, over the course of his life, he preached to more than 10 million listeners! Indeed, his influence was so great that many consider him the first celebrity in American history. His preaching shaped not only pastors, but the history of acting, drama, and performance arts. Over the middle decades of the 1700s, he did seven preaching tours around the American colonies. He even attracted Benjamin Franklin to his sermons, who was notoriously resistant to Whitefield's theology. Nevertheless, they became friends over time, and Franklin even published and distributed his sermons.

It is said that Whitefield's preaching was so rousing that Franklin made sure his pockets were empty before he went to hear him preach. One time, Franklin went knowing that an offering would be taken for an orphanage Whitefield was building in Georgia which Franklin thought a terrible idea, and had already told Whitefield as much. Here's what Franklin said after the fact:

> I had in my Pocket a Handful of Copper Money, three or four silver Dollars, and five Pistoles [Spanish coins] in Gold. As he proceeded I began to soften, and concluded to give the Coppers. Another Stroke of his Oratory made me ashamed of that, and determined me to give the Silver; and he finished so admirably, that I emptied my Pocket wholly into the Collector's Dish, Gold and all.

You can read more of Franklin's reflections on Whitefield here: http://nationalhumanitiescenter.org/pds/becomingamer/ideas/text2/franklinwhitefield.pdf.

 Richard Heitzenrater, *Wesley and the People Called Methodists*, 2nd ed. (Nashville: Abingdon Press, 2013), 109–10.

Ibid., 341.

Kevin Watson has written an excellent study on the Class meetings: *The Class Meeting: Reclaiming a Forgotten (and Essential) Small Group Experience* (Wilmore, KY: Seedbed, 2013). Kevin's book both introduces the important historical idea of a Class meeting, and helpfully discusses how we can recover this practice in the contemporary church. A second study, by Scott Kisker and Kevin Watson, gives a similar overview, background, and process for recovering the Band meeting in the present: *The Band Meeting: Rediscovering Relational Discipleship in Transformational Community* (Franklin, TN: Seedbed, 2017). As we will show in later chapters, taking up these Classes and Bands in the present is an important step in renewing the Wesleyan way. We highly recommend you consider following up this study with these two books.

The Wesleys were truly remarkable, both as authors and as editors. It's worth noting what it means to say that John Wesley was producing, and editing, all of this material. One thing Wesley felt was extremely important was the continuing education of the Methodists. He wanted to help the people under his care grow along the Wesleyan way, and part of that meant that he needed to keep supplying them with reading material that would help them understand the Wesleyan way of being a Christian. So, he would often edit together writing by other people, selecting key passages, sometimes taking out material that was irrelevant or unnecessary or potentially confusing for readers, and publish it for people to read. A lot of his publications were like this. *A Christian Library* was a collection of helpful texts he edited and published this way, for instance. Likewise, he published *Explanatory Notes* on the entire Bible. He did produce his own translations of the Bible for the text, but a lot of the material is composed of several other commentaries which he pieced together and quoted from at great length. His goal was to produce a commentary of the whole Bible that an uneducated reader could read to their benefit, and if sales are any indication, he was very successful! So, while a lot of his output was not entirely original material, anyone who has done some editing and publishing can tell you this was a truly remarkable feat, especially considering everything else Wesley had going on at the time.

LESSON 5: WHAT IS THE GOAL OF THE CHRISTIAN LIFE?

 C. S. Lewis, in his book *Mere Christianity*, makes the point this way:

> Dozens of people go to Him [God] to be cured of some one particular sin which they are ashamed of (like cowardice) or which is obviously spoiling daily life (like bad temper). Well, He will cure it all right: but He will not stop there. That may be all you asked; but if once you call Him in, He will give you the full treatment.
>
> That is why He warned people to "count the cost" before becoming Christians. "Make no mistake," He says, "if you let me, I will make you

perfect. The moment you put yourself in My hands, that is what you are in for. Nothing less, or other, than that. You have free will, and if you choose, you can push Me away. But if you do not push Me away, understand I am going to see this job through. Whatever suffering it may cost you in your earthly life, whatever inconceivable purification it may cost you in your earthly life, whatever inconceivable purification it may cost you after death, whatever it costs Me, I will never rest, nor let you rest, until you are literally perfect—until my Father can say without reservation that He is well pleased with you, as He said He was well pleased with me. This I can do and will do. But I will not do anything less. . . . God's demand for perfection need not discourage you in the least in your present attempts to be good, or even in your present failures. Each time you fall He will pick you up again. And He knows perfectly well that your own efforts are never going to bring you anywhere near perfection. On the other hand, you must realise from the outset that the goal towards which He is beginning to guide you is absolute perfection, and no power in the universe, except you yourself, can prevent Him from taking you to that goal. That is what you are in for. And it is very important to realise that. If we do not, then we are very likely to start pulling back and resisting Him after a certain point. I think that many of us, when Christ has enabled us to overcome one or two sins that were an obvious nuisance, are inclined to feel that we are now good enough. He has done all we wanted Him to do, and we should be obliged if He would now leave us alone. . . . But this is the fatal mistake. Of course we never wanted, and never asked, to be made into the sort of creatures He is going to make us into. But the question is not what we intended ourselves to be, but what He intended us to be when He made us.

C. S. Lewis, *Mere Christianity* (New York: Touchstone, 1996), 174–75.

One of the central ideas in Christian theology is that God became human so that humans might become like God. This doesn't mean, of course, that we will become all-powerful or all-knowing. If we want to understand in what way we will become like God, we look toward Jesus. Jesus Christ is the union of God and man. Though His humanity was limited, His union with God meant He was perfect. We become like Jesus specifically as we become more holy and are filled with the power and love of God. Sometimes it feels like this is impossible. This is why the incarnation of Jesus matters so much. Jesus Christ, the God-man, shows us that it is possible to become perfected in holy love.

Now, the steps we take need to be orderly. We need to get the right sequence. It's kind of like working a complicated math problem. Let's say you want to solve the problem:

$$4 + (3 \times 22 + 1)$$

How do you solve it? Do you just start at the left and move right? If so, you'll get the following:

$$4 + (3 \times 22 + 1)$$
$$= 7 \times 22 + 1$$
$$= 154 + 1$$
$$= 155$$

And you will be wrong. You have to get the steps in the right order. So we memorize the proper order of operations. We recite, "Please Excuse My Dear Aunt Sally," or PEMDAS, so we remember to work math problems with lots of different steps in the right order: (1) parenthesis, (2) exponents, (3) multiplication, (4) division, (5) addition, (6) subtraction. So:

$$4 + (3 \times 2^2 + 1)$$
$$= 4 + (3 \times 4 + 1)$$
$$= 4 + (12 + 1)$$
$$= 4 + 13$$
$$= 17$$

If that doesn't make sense to you, don't worry, the point is simply that it is really important that you get the steps in the right order. If you get the steps out of order, you may not make it to your goal. Or, at the very least, it will make things a lot harder.

LESSON 6: WHAT IS REPENTANCE?

To date, scholars have confirmed that Charles Wesley penned nearly 4,400 poems and hymns! It is said that he wrote closer to 9,000 in his lifetime, and he is widely regarded as the greatest hymn-writer in the history of Christianity. Some of his most famous hymns are "Hark! The Herald Angels Sing," "And Can It Be," "O for a Thousand Tongues to Sing," and "Love Divine, All Loves Excelling."

You can access a massive body of Charles's hymns online at https://divinity.duke. edu/initiatives/cswt/charles-published-verse.

2 A core idea in Christian theology is the concept of virtue. Virtue—according to Aristotle, who influenced Thomas Aquinas, one of the great theologians of the church—is an excellence of character. Character is something all of us have, good or bad. Good character traits are virtues. Bad character traits are vices. (Think of the seven deadly sins.) As we grow more in grace, we train our emotions to behave more in line with the truth. Behaving generously once doesn't make us a generous person, but behaving generously over a long period of time trains us to become generous people. We develop the excellent character trait—the virtue—of generosity. God doesn't want us to always do the right thing even though we hate it. He wants us to learn to love to do the right thing. When we practice the Christian faith, it should get easier and easier for us because we're becoming different people. This helps explain how it is that we can enjoy God forever. When we become heavenly people, we naturally love to do what is right!

3 In the fourth century, one of Christianity's greatest Greek theologians and church leaders, Athanasius of Alexandria, wrote a book called *On the Incarnation*. In this book, Athanasius explains why the Son became incarnate—took on flesh—in order to solve our problem. He talks about the dilemma God faced with sin. We were created with a goal of enjoying life with God forever. But as the result of sin, we find ourselves no longer moving toward eternal life, but headed toward death and corruption. God made us the kinds of creatures that would corrupt like this if we chose to turn away, and so God faced a dilemma. On the one hand, He desired us to live forever with Him, but on the other, by our choice for sin we turned away from that good order, and deserved death. Athanasius argues that the unique gift of the God-man, Jesus Christ, who is truly God and truly human, is what makes possible the overcoming of death and reordering of us back to eternal life. Because He was truly God, Jesus had the power to overcome death with immortality. Because He was truly human, Jesus had access to the problem of death, so that He could overcome it on our behalf. You can read the full argument here: Athanasius of Alexandria, *On the Incarnation*, Popular Patristics Series 44B (Yonkers, NY: St. Vladimir's Seminary Press, 2014).

LESSON 7: WHAT IS JUSTIFICATION AND NEW BIRTH?

1 If you only read one sermon by John Wesley in your life, "The Scripture Way of Salvation" is the one to read. In it, John Wesley lays out very clearly all of his thoughts on the matter of salvation. Salvation, after all, was the topic that he wrote most about, and the topic that Wesley's most important ideas all center around. However, the sermon is not only helpful for what Wesley has to teach in it about the way of salvation, but it also is a moving invitation to progress along on the way of salvation. This path and teaching are so important that we have included the sermon at the close of this volume.

Albert C. Outler, ed., *The Works of John Wesley*, Bicentennial ed., vol. 2, *Sermons II* (Nashville: Abingdon Press, 1985), 158.

2. You may notice the similarity between this story and the opening episode of Victor Hugo's novel, *Les Misérables*. In France in 1815, the main character of *Les Misérables*, Jean Valjean, is just released following a nineteen-year sentence of hard labor in prison. His original sentence was five years, for stealing bread for his starving sister. Numerous escape attempts extended his imprisonment. As a former convict, his passport prevents his admission to an inn, so he attempts to sleep on the street near the church. A woman comes along and recommends he knock on a particular door. The door is to the home of the town's bishop, Myriel, a good and modest man who is kind enough to offer him a bed for the evening. In the middle of the night, Valjean wakes, takes the bishop's silverware, and sneaks off. When the police capture Valjean, they bring him to Myriel, who pretends Valjean was given the silverware, and then adds a pair of silver candlesticks to the "gift." The police accept the explanation and leave the men. Bishop Myriel turns to Jean Valjean and says: "Never forget that you have promised me to employ this money in becoming an honest man." Jean Valjean, who had no recollection of having promised anything, stood silent. The bishop, who had laid a stress on these words, continued solemnly, "Jean Valjean, my brother, you no longer belong to evil, but to good. I have bought your soul from you. I withdraw it from black thoughts and the spirit of perdition, and give it to God." *Les Misérables* has been translated and adapted for screen and stage many times, into many languages, since its initial publication in 1862. A fine modern English translation is Victor Hugo, *Les Misérables*, trans. Norman Denny (London: Penguin Books, 1982).

3. If you are really interested in the ideas in this and the following chapters, what we are calling the way of salvation or *via salutis*, and want to learn more, two great books will give you more than enough information, including interesting points of disagreement between contemporary interpreters of Wesley's theology. Kenneth Collins (Asbury Theological Seminary) and Randy Maddox (Duke Divinity School) are two leading interpreters of John Wesley's theology, and their major works are Kenneth J. Collins, *The Theology of John Wesley: Holy Love and the Shape* *of Grace* (Nashville: Abingdon Press, 2007), and Randy L. Maddox, *Responsible Grace: John Wesley's Practical Theology* (Nashville: Kingswood Books, 1994).

LESSON 8: WHAT IS SANCTIFICATION?

1 There is a classic distinction between what theologians call "operative" and "cooperative" grace that we have been laying out here. The famous thirteenth-century theologian Thomas Aquinas makes the distinction this way: "grace may be taken in two ways; first, as a Divine help, whereby God moves us to will and to act; secondly, as a habitual gift divinely bestowed on us." (*Summa Theologiae* I–II, q. III, a. 2.)

The first sense is called operative grace, because God operates/acts on us. The second sense, cooperative, because God gives us a gift which becomes our own—we have it, which is what a habit is—and then works in partnership with our gift, so we cooperate in grace. Here Thomas is expanding on the thought of the fifth-century theologian Augustine of Hippo, who says in chapter 33 of *On Grace and Free Will*, "He operates, therefore, without us, in order that we may will; but when we will, and so will that we may act, He co-operates with us." Augustine, of course, is drawing heavily upon Paul's letter to the Romans. John Wesley gives his clearest account of this distinction, and its importance for his thought in the sermon "On Working Out Our Own Salvation," Albert Outler, ed. *The Works of John Wesley*, Bicentennial ed., vol. 3, *Sermons III* (Nashville: Abingdon Press, 1986), 199–209.

2 In the Old Testament, God gives Israel a lot of different laws to rule their life together. Go read Leviticus, and you will see all kinds of interesting parts of life that God ordered for them. For example, Leviticus 11:2–8 says:

> From among all the land animals, these are the creatures that you may eat. Any animal that has divided hoofs and is cleft-footed and chews the cud—such you may eat. But among those that chew the cud or have divided hoofs, you shall not eat the following: the camel, for even though it chews the cud, it does not have divided hoofs; it is unclean for you. The rock badger, for even though it chews the cud, it does not have divided hoofs; it is unclean for you. The hare, for even though it chews the cud, it does not have divided hoofs; it is unclean for you. The pig, for even though it has divided hoofs and is cleft-footed, it does not chew the cud; it is unclean for you. Of their flesh you shall not eat, and their carcasses you shall not touch; they are unclean for you.

Christians have not held to this teaching, although Jews have (hence, they do not eat pork). The question is, of course, why? Didn't Jesus say, "I have come not to abolish [the law] but to fulfill [it]" (Matt. 5:17)?

A usual strategy for answering these questions is to distinguish between different parts of the Old Testament law. This was the strategy preferred by John Wesley, as it was for his church. When Wesley sent Articles of Religion to Methodists in America, he included an article on the law. It reads:

> Article VI—Of the Old Testament
> The Old Testament is not contrary to the New; for both in the Old and New Testament everlasting life is offered to mankind by Christ, who is the only Mediator between God and man, being both God and Man. Wherefore they are not to be heard who feign that the old fathers did look only for transitory promises. Although the law given from God by Moses as touching ceremonies and rites doth not bind Christians, nor ought the civil precepts thereof of necessity be received in any common-wealth; yet notwithstanding, no Christian whatsoever is free from the obedience of the commandments which are called moral.

In the last sentence, the article distinguishes between the ceremonial law, the civil law, and the moral law given in the Old Testament. Only the last law holds for Christians. However, the principle that God cares about our ceremonies (including diets) and our life as a civil society holds. John Wesley confirmed this basic outlook in his sermon, "The Original, Nature, Property, and Use of the Law." Albert Outler, ed. *The Works of John Wesley*, Bicentennial ed., vol. 2, *Sermons II* (Nashville, Abingdon Press, 1985), 4–19.

John Wesley wrote several treatises over the course of his life on the topic of Christian perfection, an issue we will discuss in more detail in the next chapter. Our definition of sin here is drawn from those texts taken together, which describe the process of becoming holy, sanctified, or perfect (all synonyms for Wesley) as a twofold process of dying to sin and growing in grace. The idea that grace pushes out and replaces sin, and that process of pushing out deeper and deeper layers of sin, pushing it out by filling the soul deeper and deeper with the stronger power of grace, is sanctification. You can read all of John Wesley's key writings on Christian perfection, along with a helpful introduction to the doctrine's background and development, in Paul Wesley Chilcote and Kenneth J. Collins, eds., *The Works of John Wesley*, Bicentennial ed., vol. 13, *Doctrinal and Controversial Treatises II* (Nashville: Abingdon Press, 2013), 1–199.

 C. S. Lewis, *Mere Christianity* (New York: Touchstone, 1996), 176.

LESSON 9: WHAT IS ENTIRE SANCTIFICATION?

One key text for teaching about Christian perfection in the Wesleyan tradition is 1 John. John Wesley repeatedly cites 1 John 4 when teaching about Christian perfection, especially on the connection between Christian perfection and perfect love, as in 1 John 4:16–19:

> God is love, and those who abide in love abide in God, and God abides in them. Love has been perfected among us in this: that we may have boldness on the day of judgment, because as he is, so are we in this world. There is no fear in love, but perfect love casts out fear; for fear has to do with punishment, and whoever fears has not reached perfection in love. We love because he first loved us.

First John has remained a key text in the Wesleyan tradition. One of our very finest theologians, William Burt Pope, made this letter the centerpiece of his theology. One of his finest sermons, "The Inner Witness of Life in the Son," is well worth reading in this connection. You can read the sermon in William Burt Pope, *The Inward Witness and Other Discourses* (London: Ballantyne Press, 1885), 1–31. The text is available for free as an electronic copy many places online.

 See Lesson 1 for the story of John Wesley at sea with the German Moravians.

John Wesley summarized his thoughts on the topic of Christian perfection in eleven points near the conclusion of his treatise "A Plain Account of Christian Perfection." Those points are:

1. There is such a thing as *perfection*; for it is again and again mentioned in Scripture.

2. It is not so early as justification; for justified persons are to "go on to perfection."

3. It is not so late as death; for St. Paul speaks of living men that were perfect.

4. It is not *absolute*. Absolute perfection belongs not to man—no, nor to angels; but to God alone.

5. It does not make a man infallible—none is infallible while he remains in the body.

6. Is it *sinless*? It is not worthwhile to contend for a term. It is salvation from sin.

7. It is *perfect love*. This is the essence of it. Its properties, or inseparable fruits, are "rejoicing evermore," "praying without ceasing," and "in everything giving thanks."

8. It is *improvable*. It is so far from lying in an indivisible point, from being incapable of increase, that one perfected in love may grow in grace far swifter than he did before.

9. It is *amissable*, capable of being lost; of which we have numerous instances. But we were not thoroughly convinced of this till five or six years ago.

10. It is constantly both preceded and followed by a *gradual* work.

Finally, as an eleventh point, Wesley ponders for some time whether Christian perfection is "in itself instantaneous, or not." He concludes that is it, in fact, instantaneous, and that this fact is the very thing which makes the preaching of Christian perfection so important.

You can read the whole treatise here: Paul Wesley Chilcote and Kenneth J. Collins, eds., *The Works of John Wesley*, Bicentennial ed., vol. 13, *Doctrinal and Controversial Treatises II* (Nashville: Abingdon Press, 2013), 132–91.

Here is a famous account of the experience of Christian perfection by Jane Cooper, published here and there by John Wesley, that gives some glimpse of what this rest looks like:

> I was in a moment enabled to lay hold on Jesus Christ, and found salvation by simple faith. He assured me, the Lord, the King, was in the midst of me, and that I should see evil no more. I now blessed him who had visited and redeemed me, and was become my "wisdom, righteousness, sanctification, and redemption." I saw Jesus altogether lovely, and knew he was mine in all his offices. And, glory be to him! He now reigns in my heart without a rival. I find no will but his. I feel no pride; nor any affection but what is placed on him.

Wesley also published extracts from the journal of another woman, Elizabeth Harper, who also experienced Christian perfection, or entire sanctification, but shows that this did not mean her life went perfectly. Wesley underscored this point in his note to the reader at the opening of the extracts, when he wrote:

> To set the doctrine of Christian perfection too high is the ready way to drive it out of the world. Let a man only describe it as implying a freedom from mistakes and human infirmities, and whoever knows there is no such freedom in this life naturally concludes, "There is no perfection." Hence we should always carefully guard against this, by insisting, it is no more and no less than giving God all our heart; loving him with all our heart, and our neighbor as ourselves. This is well consistent with a thousand infirmities, which belong to every soul while in the body.

Chilcote and Collins, eds., *Doctrinal and Controversial Treatises II*, 183–84, 194.

Timothy Tennant gives a nice explanation of entire sanctification and holiness in *The Call to Holiness: Pursuing the Heart of God for the Love of the World* (Franklin, TN: Seedbed, 2014).

LESSON 10: WHAT ARE SACRAMENTS?

A common way of thinking about the spiritual disciplines is to divide them up as works of mercy and works of piety. Works of mercy are aimed outward at the wider world: giving to the poor, working to end social injustices, caring for people in distress, and other acts of service. Works of piety are aimed inward, at the community or at the individual. Scripture study, prayer, and fasting, either alone or in community, all help us to grow closer to God.

Wesleyans believe that sacraments (baptism and Communion) are both signs and things. Article 16 of the Articles of Religion, which you can find in the *Book of Discipline of the United Methodist Church*, among other places, is on the sacraments, and states that "Sacraments ordained of Christ are not only badges or tokens of Christian men's profession, but rather they are certain signs of grace, and God's good will toward us, by which he doth work invisibly in us, and doth not only quicken, but also strengthen and confirm, our faith in him." They are signs, and not only that, but the kinds of signs "by which God does work in us." This is what we mean by "signs and things." It is important to keep both these ideas in mind. The Wesleyan answer to "what is a sacrament" isn't an only, but a both. While a majority of evangelical Protestants in America answer that they are only signs, or memorials (nondenominational churches and many Baptists hold to this view, for instance), we Wesleyans say, "Yes, they are certain signs which remind us of God and grace, but they are also the means whereby the thing itself—the grace itself—is given to us!"

3 Historically, Wesleyans have practiced infant baptism. Recall that John Wesley was a priest in the Church of England, what we think of as the Episcopal or Anglican church in the United States. We have, historically, retained this practice. For those baptized as infants, we usually practice a later ceremony of confirmation, which is like, yet unlike, baptism. There, the one who was baptized as an infant is confirmed in the faith. One thing that always happens at a baptism is that there is a profession of faith before the water is applied. This is usually done by a series of questions and answers. The pastor asks: "Do you confess Jesus Christ as your Savior, put your whole trust in His grace, and promise to serve Him as your Lord, in union with the church which Christ has opened to people of all ages, nations, and races?" And someone responds: "I do." If the child cannot answer (after all, infants cannot really converse), then the parents answer on behalf of the child. But later, at another ceremony similar to the baptism ceremony, a young person who was baptized as an infant will stand up before the congregation and make their own profession. They will *confirm* the faith that was spoken for them by their parents.

4 *The United Methodist Hymnal: Book of United Methodist Worship* (Nashville: United Methodist Publishing House, 1989), 10.

5 Christians have long debated whether and how it is that Jesus Christ is present in the bread and wine at the Lord's Supper. Some have said that the substance of the bread and wine are converted, changed into the substance of Christ's body and blood. We call this view *transubstantiation*, and it is has been taught by the Roman Catholic Church since at least the Middle Ages. Others want to say that while the substance isn't changed and what remains is substantially bread and wine, nevertheless the substance of Christ's body and blood is there with the bread and wine. We call this *consubstantiation*, and it is the official teaching of the Lutheran churches. Wesleyans follow the teaching of John Calvin, who influenced the Church of England. We teach the mystery of Christ's "real presence." That is, while we insist that Christ is really present in the Lord's Supper, we hold back from any particular theory of how it is, metaphysically, that Christ is really present. We insist, however, that Christ is really, spiritually present, and we really receive the grace of union to God through our union to Christ. A great book on the Methodist position on this issue is Kenneth M. Loyer, *Holy Communion: Celebrating God with Us* (Nashville: Abingdon Press, 2014).

LESSON 11: WHAT ARE CLASSES AND BANDS?

 We've slightly adjusted the basic idea, but it comes from Dorotheos of Gaza. Dorotheos writes:

> Suppose we were to take a compass and insert the point and draw the outline of a circle. The center point is the same distance from any point on the circumference. . . . Let us suppose that this circle is the world and that God himself is the center: the straight lines drawn from the circumference to the center are the lives of human beings. . . . Let us assume for the sake of the analogy that to move toward God, then, human beings move from the circumference along the various radii of the circle to the center. But at the same time, the closer they are to God, the closer they become to one another; and the closer they are to one another, the closer they become to God.

You can find the quote, and a longer description of the idea in early Christian monasticism, in Roberta Bondi, *To Love as God Loves: Conversations with the Early Church* (Philadelphia: Fortress Press, 1987), 25.

The Class, for the early Methodists, was for anyone "who desires to flee the wrath of God," to use John Wesley's language. To use our language in this book, it is for anyone in a state of repentance. Take a look back at chapter 6. Recall the Island of Blurry Vision. The Class for Blurry Vision would not be for people who think their vision is just fine, but it's also not *only* for people who have had their vision corrected. It's for anyone who has come to the realization that their vision is bad, and desires to have it fixed. On the Wesleyan way, the Class is for those who have realized they are sinners and need to be healed as well as those who have been healed. John Wesley described the purpose of these Societies, comprised of members of the Classes, as follows: "Such a Society is no other than a company of men 'having the form, and seeking the power of godliness,' united in order to pray together, to receive the word of exhortation, and to watch over one another in love, that they may help each other to work out their salvation."

In early Methodism, these Classes were led by the Class leader, a very important role in the history of Methodism. Wesley assigned three General Rules for the leaders and members of these Classes, which are summarized as follows:

1. Doing no harm, avoiding evil in every kind—especially that which is most generally practiced.

2. Doing good, by being very kind and merciful after their power, as they have opportunity doing good of every possible sort and as far as is possible to all men.

3. Attending upon all the ordinances of God.

Wesley gives some pretty detailed account of what is involved for each of these three General Rules. You can read about it here: Rupert E. Davies, ed., *The Works of John Wesley*, Bicentennial ed., vol. 9, *The Methodist Societies: History, Nature, and Design* (Nashville: Abingdon Press, 1989), 67–75.

3. Notice how thorough this series of questions is. First, you ask what known sins you have committed. The expectation is that you are reflecting upon, coming to notice, and think about the sin in your life. Over time, the longer you attend a Band meeting, the more aware you become of sin in your life. Likewise, you become better aware of temptations (question two), and come to notice how it is that you both fail to resist temptations (which you confess in question one) or else are delivered from temptation (which you recount in question three). The language of "delivered" is theologically important, because we have noted that we are powerless in the face of sin, and it is only by the power of God that we are delivered from it. Finally, there are those things which we may not be sure about. Was it a sin to forget a part of my homework this week because I was too tired after my basketball game? Even that stuff needs to be brought into the light and have the community offer its wisdom. And, finally, the hardest, fifth question asks if there is anything you would like to keep secret. That is, is there anything you know or think is sin that you aren't ready to confess yet? You may not confess it this week, but answering the question honestly will build strength to confess even those most hidden sins over time. So you can see, these questions are thorough, and take seriously how thorough our problem of sin is. These are serious questions, and the key to practicing them is keeping them serious, and honestly answering them. No surprise this was the most intense group in Methodism!

LESSON 12: WHAT HAPPENED AFTER WESLEY?

1 All these numbers are taken from essays in Emory Stevens Bucke, ed., *The History of American Methodism*, 3 vols. (Nashville: Abingdon Press, 1964). For more on the history of American Methodism, see Russell E. Richey, Kenneth E. Rowe, and Jean Miller Schmidt, eds. *American Methodism: A Compact History* (Nashville: Abingdon Press, 2012) and *The Methodist Experience in America*, 2 vols. (Nashville: Abingdon Press, 2000–10).

2 Methodists have long exhibited pride over the relationship between John Wesley and William Wilberforce, the man who spearheaded the abolition of slave trade in England. Wesley was a vocal supporter of Wilberforce and advocate of the abolition of the English slave trade. Wilberforce's efforts have been recounted in the film *Amazing Grace*, based on Wilberforce's biography, written by Eric Metaxas: *Amazing Grace: William Wilberforce and the Heroic Campaign to End Slavery* (New York: HarperOne, 2007). In the last year of Wesley's life, Wesley wrote to Wilberforce, encouraging him to "go on, in the name of God and in the power of his might, till even American slavery (the vilest that ever saw the sun) shall vanish away before it." John Telford, ed. *The Letters of the Rev. John Wesley*, vol. 8 (London: Epworth Press, 1931), 265. Of course, the history of Methodism and slavery in America was exceedingly complicated, as it led to the division of the Methodist church into two: in the North, the Methodist Episcopal Church (MEC), and in the South, the Methodist Episcopal Church, South (MEC, South).

3 The authoritative biography of Francis Asbury, which will tell you more than you could ever want to know about the great leader of early American Methodism, is by John Wigger, *American Saint: Francis Asbury and the Methodists* (Oxford: Oxford University Press, 2009).

4 Again, check out the books by Kevin Watson and Scott Kisker. A good path would be to begin with Watson's *The Class Meeting*. Then, once you have a good group together and have been running a Class for a bit, see if anyone wants to move on into a Band. Bands should be smaller—3 or 4—and male or female only. The book by Watson and Kisker, *The Band Meeting*, will walk you through a great process for forming a Band. Above all, look for people to walk with you along the Wesleyan way. The Christian life can be lonely, but it doesn't have to be.

5 Thomas Jackson, ed., *The Works of John Wesley*, vol. 13 (London: Conference Office, 1879), 258.

For more teaching resources that go with this book, please visit
seedbed.com/absolutebasics